SCHOOLS
WHERE
CHILDREN
LEARN

Joseph Featherstone

SCHOOLS WHERE CHILDREN LEARN

 LIVERIGHT
NEW YORK

1.987654321

SBN: 87140–524–5
Library of Congress Catalog Card Number: 75–148664

Designed by Charlotte Thorp

Manufactured in the United States of America

CONTENTS

Preface

All these essays represent ongoing journalistic work; I've had to cut some repetitive material, and make some changes here and there; but mostly I've left them substantially the same as they first appeared. The Talent Corps is now a community college; the street academy program in Harlem is a more diffuse and, in some respects, less interesting operation; and there are now a handful, instead of two, Roxbury community schools. Time has thus outdistanced some of these pieces, although I hope they are still of general interest.

I owe a great debt to Gilbert Harrison, the editor of *The New Republic*, who, among other things, indulges my obsessions. Also to David and Frances Hawkins, Tony

Kallet, Maurice Kogan, Marjorie Martus, and Rosemary Williams, for help, advice, and example. My wife, Helen, is the real teacher.

Introduction

These pieces on schools, learning, and teaching have appeared in *The New Republic* over the last three years. As I reread them, it seems to me that many share an implicit theme: the necessity for establishing standards. By standards, I don't mean crudely mechanical check-lists or standardized national tests but rather a common conviction about what it means to do a good job. The most impressive achievement of the English primary schools is the feeling on the part of teachers that they are participating in a common enterprise, working out, from classroom experience, what may one day be articulated as a sound philosophy of education. A healthy profession possesses a certain

number of such guiding ideas; the absence of them in our
schools is a symptom of professional malaise.

Only two of these essays touch directly on the pathological professionalism of our educators. One is a report on
a California bill that is now law in that state; the other a
sketch of the remarkable Talent Corps. Both are concerned
with small possibilities for opening up new pathways into
the profession and shifting training to actual classroom experience. Credentials are only a small first step, however.
Were I rewriting these pieces, I would insist that the bureaucratic sickness of the education profession is only an
extreme instance of a more general disease afflicting other
professions as well, notably medicine and law. The cure is
the same for all: to replace the unresponsive hierarchies
that now exist mainly to serve entrenched interests with
new, humane professions that really serve their clients, particularly poor clients. It is too early to tell what will become of the movement for community control of schools
and other institutions, but its fate is also bound up with
the possibilities of a new professionalism.

These are the issues I would write about today. While
writing most of these articles, though, I was concerned with
more narrow, perhaps equally important questions—
questions that will no doubt persist under any social order:
what are good settings for learning? what kinds of things
should be learned in early years of school? are there working examples of good schools on any mass scale?

There are dangers in writing within such a narrow com-
pass: the danger of becoming remote from our everyday
sense of the workings of ordinary schools, the weakness of
ignoring most of the disparate social and personal chemis-
tries that make for a promising learning environment, the
risk of talking about one style of teaching as though it
were the only effective way to teach. I'm especially anxious

to avoid leaving readers with the impression that one can single out a few elements of a good school—children's writing, the physical layout of an infant school classroom—and turn them into a formula to impose on teachers and children in other schools. There is, we will have to learn, no technical solution, no single lever to pull and cause good schools to come into being. Realizing this, we can then work slowly toward a vision of the kind of learning we wish to promote. That, among other things, is a matter of choosing what we value.

Certainly it would be sentimental to speak of improving values, attitudes, and approaches of teachers without also acknowledging that much that is wrong with our schools stems from fundamental defects in American life. There is more than one kind of sentimentality, though, and radical appeals for fundamental change have a way of turning easy substitutes for thought, work, and action. I believe that in some places, at certain levels, the educational system is ripe for change. For example, it seems to me that the elementary schools are fertile ground for new doctrines; the graduate schools, by contrast, continue to harden their formidable cake of custom, inertia, and smug self-interest.

The pity of the present moment in American education is that the air is filled with a kind of sociological determinism about schools; when breathed, it inspires the most profound fatalism. "Schools reflect social forces," the experts sigh. "The margins for maneuvering are very slight, perhaps nonexistent. We need more research." In some ways, this gloom is a refreshing departure from the traditional American notion that schools alone can remedy the damage done to children and their families by an unjust and racist society. That was always silly. The lessons slum schools teach their students are never going to be as vivid as the lessons they learn from existence in the slums. This

will remain so even after our ghetto schools end their present intolerable aloofness from the communities around
them.

However, the work of good British primary schools
suggests that change is possible within the limits of a social
order that is nearly as unsatisfactory as our own. All
schooling, the boys of Barbiana, Italy have written, is a
"war against the poor," and English schools are no exception, particularly those at the secondary level and in slum
and immigrant areas. There is nothing in England's placid
political life to compare with the ferment in America over
race, equality, and issues like community control. Nonetheless, visitors to scattered industrial and immigrant areas of
Britain have noted large numbers of primary schools doing
an exemplary job with the children of the poor and the
working classes. England remains, like America, a caste-
ridden capitalist nation; the millenium is far away. Yet, a
comparable change in our schools would mean a great deal
for the quality of our children's lives.

PART ONE

THE
PRIMARY SCHOOL
REVOLUTION
IN BRITAIN

Commentary

One point enthusiasts who visit England are apt to neglect is the limits of what has been accomplished in England so far. After some thirty years of reform, British teachers are still underpaid, classrooms are more crowded than ours, and school buildings are smelly, antique monstrosities. In some areas the prospects for stable reform have been wiped out by appalling turnovers in staff. There are plenty of wretched schools in England; good English schools tend to cluster in a few local authorities where reform has taken solid roots, becoming itself something of an orthodoxy. As I note in Chapter 1, judged by the vague but discernible standards of a governmental study (the Plowden Report) entitled *Children and Their Primary Schools,** only about a third of the country's primary schools are good, and the change is most widespread in the infant schools; in general, reform faces more obstacles the higher up the educational ladder you go. English secondary schools may be in even worse shape than our high schools.

So much for the limits of reform, which are real enough. Certain prerequisites should also be kept in mind. One ought to be of special interest to Americans now that early childhood and preschool programs are coming in for so much attention. This is the traditional conviction of British infant school teachers that young children have distinct educational needs. English teachers are inclined to relate their teaching to theories of child development stressing individual learning and learning in what David Hawkins has called the concrete mode—messing around with stuff. As is indicated in Chapter 1, the characteristic innovations of the primary school revolution first appeared in nursery schools influenced by followers of Montessori, Susan Isaacs, Dewey, and Piaget. This profound influence of preschool traditions on practices in later grades is just the opposite of what has happened in this country where good preschools have often been bullied into becoming prep schools for inflexible first-grade classes. Another prerequisite is the autonomy granted principals and teachers within the decentralized British educational system. This relative independence affects the quality of all relationships within the system. (It also makes English schools too remote from parents, a point which many good English principals concede.) Americans need to learn about the work of a class of people, the national and local inspectorates and advisory groups, whose main function is to help people do a better job—their precise role is

*The Plowden Committee, *Children and Their Primary Schools*, Her Majesty's Stationery Office, 1967.

hard to describe. The archetype of the class are the HMIs, the government inspectors. Lillian Weber, Rosemary Williams, and Lore Rasmussen are all attempting variants of this advisory role in the United States: it will be important if they can develop people with the necessary tact and skills—experienced in informal teaching and able to assist teachers without bossing them around.

It would be helpful, too, if Americans—and especially the social scientists and academics dominating our discussions of schools—understood something of the relationship between theory and practice in the English reform. As I explain, developmental theory, particularly the work of Piaget, the Swiss psychologist, provides theoretical justification for some of the methods of the infant schools, notably in mathematics. Part II of the Plowden Report, *The Growth of the Child*, shows this theoretical influence at work in its impressive arguments for the proposition that each child develops at a separate pace and that this ought to be reflected in patterns of teaching. Behind the new view of what constitutes a proper primary school curriculum (see Part V of the Plowden Report, the heart of the document) there is a definite theory of teaching. It lays a special stress on:

> . . . individual discovery, on first-hand experience and on opportunities for creative work. It insists that knowledge does not fall in neatly separate compartments and that work and play are not opposite, but complementary.

Yet, while a body of intertwined psychological theory and pedagogical practice is slowly emerging in England, we should note another point the report emphasizes: principals and teachers of schools most successful in practice are sometimes unable to formulate their aims clearly and convincingly. Theory does matter, but it can only be of practical use when it has a living relationship with teachers and children functioning in real classrooms. Without this connection to the realm of practice, theories become dead and sterile. Piaget is fortunate in that much of the British teachers' practical work intersects with his theoretical concerns. He has fared better than John Dewey, whose ideas often fell on stony pedagogical soil.

The existence of a body of good work is in itself important in spreading further good work. One way an inexperienced teacher can gain the necessary confidence in children's learning abilities and her own ability to teach informally is by operating for a time in a good informal setting under the guidance of an experienced teacher. That is how teachers ought to get their training. The satisfaction of successfully turning a classroom into a good learning environment gives teachers new confidence in their own judgments. Teachers I've spoken to report that the quality and variety of the children's work over a period of time confirmed their instinctive feeling that there ought to be other standards besides conventional achievement and IQ tests. England's is a test-ridden educational system, and it is therefore doubly interesting to see the way in which a solid body of excellent work in areas like math, writing, movement, and art is confirming principals and teachers in their reluctance to let crude quantitative test scores determine decisions concerning the education of young children (however much they may continue to determine the fate of older English children).

Specific qualitative concerns—such as what makes a school good—are lacking in most of our discussions of education, as are specific accounts of children's learning. Partly this reflects the grandiose mentality of school managers and reformers who are seldom interested in pedagogy anyway; partly it reflects the influence of quantitative social science. James Coleman's report "Equality of Educational Opportunity" marked an impressive advance in knowledge, but it seems to me characteristic of a prevailing cast of thought that Mr. Coleman and his colleagues were not particularly interested in doing qualitative studies of schools that succeeded—for instance, ghetto schools whose black pupils were scoring unexpectedly well on the tests. With due respect to quantitative research—there is, after all, so much more we need to know about the schools—I think it unlikely that we will find out how good schools succeed by continuing to submit relatively crude and undigested data to increasingly refined statistical manipulation.

The English themselves are only beginning to think in any analytic way about good schools. The Plowden Report at one point cites 109 superb schools and then more or less drops the subject. But why are those schools so good? And why aren't there more? David Hawkins has noted that you often visit infant schools in England where the standard materials and basic organization are all there, but where the teacher is merely coping, managing the room well enough without particularly responding to individual children. Frequently such classrooms are better than our formal classrooms—the children may be actively involved with materials, after all—but they are different from settings in which the teacher is watching the children closely and knows when to intervene, change the pace, ask a question, or make a suggestion for the greatest pedagogical advantage. It would be a great help if such differences could be described in terms accessible to working teachers; like learning, teaching is still pretty largely a mysterious business, and our ideas about the difference between effective and ineffectual teaching are hazy at best. A concern for these distinctions is, it seems to me, one of the features of a healthy reform movement.

CHAPTER 1

INFANT SCHOOLS

"The Integrated Day"

My wife and I had been told about good things happening in British classrooms, but we were scarcely prepared for what we found; in recent decades there has been a profound and sweeping revolution in English primary education, involving new ways of thinking about how young children learn, classroom organization, the curriculum, and the role of the teacher. We saw schools in some good local educational authorities—Bristol, Nottingham, Leicestershire, Oxfordshire—and a few serving immigrant areas in cities like London.

In what follows, I'm going to be as specific as I can

about how classes work, how the room is laid out, what sort of things are in it, how the teacher and the children spend the day, and, in some detail, how a child learns to read, as an example of the kind of learning that goes on. I know that American teachers, particularly good ones, are rightly suspicious of most talk on education, because so little of what they hear relates to actual classroom practice. I hope I can be concrete enough. The relevance of these British classrooms to American education is a difficult question which I'll leave for later.

Primary schools in Britain divide into "infant" and "junior" schools. The infant schools in England take the children from the age of five to seven, and in some authorities, eight. It is in the infant schools that people learn to read and write and to work with numbers. Junior schools take children from seven or eight to eleven, and in some places twelve; they then go on to secondary school. Infant and junior schools sometimes occupy the same building, and some authorities—Oxfordshire, for example—have a policy of putting them together in one unit, like an American elementary school.

It is important to understand that what goes on in good infant schools is much the same. The approach is similar, though the quality of teaching and children's work varies greatly.

Westfield Infant School, for example, is a one-story structure, like any of a thousand American buildings, on a working-class housing estate in Leicestershire. If you arrive early, you find a number of children already inside, reading, writing, painting, playing music, tending to pets. Teachers sift in slowly and begin working with students. Apart from a religious assembly (required by law), it's hard to say just when school actually begins because there is very little organized activity for a whole class. The puzzled visitor sees some small group work in mathematics ("maths") or reading, but mostly children are on their own, moving about and talking quite freely. The teacher sometimes sits at her desk, and the children flock to her for consultations, but more often she moves about the room, advising on projects, listening to children read, asking questions, giving words, talking, sometimes prodding.

The hallways, which are about the size of those in American schools, are filled with busy children, displays of paintings and graphs, a grocery store where children use play money and learn to count, easels, tables for collections of shells and plants, workbenches on which to pound and hammer nails and boards, big wooden boxes full of building blocks.

Classrooms open out onto the playground, which is also much in use. A contingent of children is kneeling on the grass, clocking the speed of a tortoise, which they want to graph against the speeds of other pets, and of people. Nearby are five-year-olds, finishing an intricate, tall tower of blocks, triumphantly counting as they add the last one, "twenty three, twenty four." A solitary boy is mixing powders for paint; on a large piece of paper attached to an easel, with very big strokes, he makes an ominous, stylized building that seems largely to consist of black shutters framing deep red windows. "It's the hospital where my brother is," he explains and pulls the visitor over to the class-library corner where a picture book discusses hospitals. He can't read it yet (he's five) but says he is trying. And he is; he can make out a number of words, some pretty hard, on different pages, and it is clear that he has been *studying* the book, because he wants badly to know about hospitals. At another end of the hall there is a quieter library nook for the whole school. Here two small boys are reading aloud; the better reader is, with indifferent grace, correcting the grateful slower boy as he stumbles over words.

The rooms are fairly noisy—more noisy than many American teachers or principals would allow—because children can talk freely. Sometimes the teacher has to ask for quiet. With as many as forty in some classes, rooms are crowded and accidents happen. Paint spills, a tub overflows, there are recriminations. Usually the children mop up and work resumes.

The visitor is dazed by the amount and variety and fluency of free writing produced: stories, free-verse poems with intricate images, precise accounts of experiments in "maths" and, finally, looking over a tiny little girl's shoulder, he finds: "Today we had visitors from America. . . ."

After a time, you overcome your confusion at the sheer variety of it all, and you begin making more definite observations. The physical layout of the classrooms is markedly different. American teachers are coming to appreciate the importance of a flexible room, but even in good elementary schools in the United States this usually means having movable, rather than fixed, desks. In the Westfield School there are no individual desks and no assigned places. Around the room (which is about the size of one you would find in an average American school) there are different tables for different activities: art, water and sand play, number work. The number tables have all kinds of number lines—strips of paper with numbers marked on them in sequence; on these children learn to count and reason mathematically. There are beads, buttons, and odd things to count; weights and balances; dry and liquid measures; and a rich variety of apparatus for learning basic mathematical concepts, some of it home-made, some ready-made. The best of the commercial materials are familiar: Cuisenaire rods, the Dienes multibase material, Stern rods, and attribute or logical blocks. This sort of thing is stressed much more than formal arithmetic.

Every class has a library alcove, separated off by a room divider that also serves as a display shelf for books. Some library corners have a patch of carpet and an old easy chair. Every room has a "Wendy House," a play corner with dolls and furniture for playing house. Often there is a dress-up corner, too, with different kinds of cast-off adult clothes. The small children love the Wendy houses and dress-up corners, but you see older ones using them as well. Some classes have puppet theaters for putting on improvised plays with homemade puppets—although many make do with the legs of one table turned upside down on top of another for a makeshift stage. Often, small children perform dance dramas involving a lot of motion and a minimum of words.

Gradually it becomes clear how the day proceeds in one of these rooms. In many infant and some junior schools the choice of the day's routine is left completely up to the teacher; the teacher, in turn, leaves options open to the children. Classes for young children are reaching a point in many schools where there is no real difference between one subject in the curriculum and another, or even between work and play. A school day run on these lines is called, variously, the "free day," the "integrated curriculum," or the "integrated day." The term scarcely matters.

In a school that operates on the integrated day, the teacher usually starts the morning by listing the different activities available. A good deal of material is needed, according to the teachers, but the best of it is often homemade; in any case, it isn't necessary to have thirty or forty sets of everything, because most activities are for a limited number of people. "Six Children Can Play in the Wendy House," says a sign in one classroom. The ground rules are that they must clean up when they finish and they mustn't bother others.

A child might spend the day on his first choice, or he might not. Many teachers confess they get nervous if everybody doesn't do some reading and writing every day; others are committed in principle to letting children choose freely. In practice, many teachers give work when they think it's needed. In this, as in any other way of doing things, teachers tailor their styles to their own temperaments and to those of the children. But the extent to which children really have a choice and really work purposefully is astonishing.

How they learn reading offers an example of the kind of individual learning and teaching going on in these classrooms, even in quite large ones. (The mathematics work shows this even better, but that will be described later.) Reading is not particularly emphasized, and my purpose in singling it out is purely illustrative, though the contrast between English classes and most American ones, where reading is a formidable matter, is vivid and depressing.

At first it is hard to say just how they do learn to read since there are no separate subjects. A part of the answer slowly becomes clear, and it surprises American visitors used to thinking of the teacher as the generating force of education: children learn from each other. They hang around the library corners long before they can read, handling the books, looking at pictures, trying to find words they do know, listening and watching as the teacher hears other children's reading. It is common to see nonreaders studying people as they read, and then imitating them, monkey doing what monkey sees. Nobody makes fun of their grave parodies, and for good reasons.

A very small number of schools in two or three authorities have adopted what they call "family" or "vertical" grouping, which further promotes the idea of children teaching children. In these schools, each class is a cross section of the whole school's population, all ages mixed together. This seems particularly successful in the early school years, when newcomers are easily absorbed, and older children help teach the young ones to clean up and take first steps in reading. The older children, too, benefit from classroom environment where they can occasionally be babyish; they also learn a good deal from the role of teacher they adopt. Family grouping needs smaller classes, teachers say, because it requires close supervision to make sure small children don't get overshadowed and big ones are still challenged. Teachers using family grouping swear by the flexibility it provides.

A range of reading schemes is used: sight reading, phonics, and so forth, whatever seems to work with a child. (Only about five percent of British schools use the Initial Teaching Alphabet—an improved alphabet, not a method of reading—that has proved successful with poor readers and adults both in England and in this country; principals of good schools we visited thought that ITA was unnecessary with a truly flexible reading program, but that in a rigid scheme it gave the slow reader another chance, and thus a break.) Increasingly in the better infant schools, there are no textbooks and no class readers, just books, in profusion. Instead of spending their scanty book money on forty sets of everything, schools have purchased different sets of reading series, as well as a great many single books, at all levels of difficulty. Teachers arrange their classroom libraries so they can direct students of different abilities to appropriate books, but in most classes a child can tackle anything he wants. As a check, cautious teachers ask them to go on their own through a graded reading series—which one doesn't matter.

However a child picks up reading, it will involve learning to write at the same time, and some write before they
can read; there is an attempt to break down the mental
barrier between the spoken, the written, and the printed
word. When a child starts school, he gets a large, unlined
notebook; this is his book for free writing, and he can put
what he wants in it. On his own, he may draw a picture in
it with crayon or pencil, discuss the picture with the teacher, and dictate a caption to her, which she then writes
down for him: "This is my Dad." He copies the caption,
writing just underneath. In this way he learns to memorize
the look and sound of his dictated words and phrases until
he reaches a point where, with help, he can write sentences.
Often his notebook serves as his own first reading book.

He also gets a smaller notebook, his private dictionary,
in which he enters words as he learns them. "I got a new
word," a five-year-old brags to the visitor. Children are always running to the teacher for words as they find they
have more and more to write. Good teachers don't give in
without a struggle: the children have to guess the first letter and sound the word out before they get it. Thus they
pick up phonetic skills informally, although some teachers
do use sight cards and some formal phonics work. Gradually as a child amasses a reading and writing vocabulary, he
reaches a fluent stage and you see six-year-olds writing
stories, free-verse poems, accounts of things done in class,
for an audience that includes other children as well as the
teacher.

As a rule, teachers don't pay much attention to ac-
curacy or neatness until a child is well on in his writing.
They introduce grammar and spelling after a time, but not
as separate subjects or ends in themselves. They are simply
ways to say what you want more efficiently. Under these
methods, where the children choose the content of their

writing, more attention is paid to content than externals such as punctuation, spelling, and grammar. In good schools these are presented as what they are: living ways to get a meaning across, to be understood. Even unimaginative teachers, who quibble with children about other work, can learn to respect the content of the free writing books and take it seriously. This emphasis on self-chosen content has produced a flowering of young children's literature in schools working with many kinds of teachers and children. There is growing recognition that different people flourish on different kinds of writing; storytellers and poets are not necessarily the same as those who can do elegant and graceful writing about mathematics. Impressive examples of free writing and poetry similar to what we saw are contained in the West Riding Education Committee's anthology, *The Excitement of Writing.** Samples of "maths" writing are included in the Schools Council's *Mathematics in the Primary Schools*, a wonderfully instructive book on many accounts.** Books made and illustrated by the children are coming to be a regular part of the curriculum in some schools.

Informal Schools

Of course children spend their time doing things other than reading, and the teachers in the schools we saw would be annoyed at the manner in which I've singled out one academic subject. The very best often argue that art is the key. The head of Sea Mills School in Bristol believes firmly that if the art is good, all else follows. All else does follow, richly, at Sea Mills, where the infants sat us down and

---

* See pp. 49-50 for some excerpts from this book.

**Schools Council's Council Curriculum bulletin no. 1, *Mathematics in the Primary Schools,* Her Majesty's Stationery Office, 1966.

performed a concert of skillful poetry and songs they had made up.

But my purpose was to show not reading methods but the changed role of the teacher. Formal classroom teaching —the instructor standing up front, talking to the group, or even the first-grade room divided up into reading groups which the teacher listens to separately as she tries desperately to keep order—has disappeared because it imposes a single pattern of learning on a whole group of children (thus forcing the schools to "track," or to group classes by ability), because it ignores the extent to which children teach each other, and because in many workaday schools other methods are proving to be better. Ordinary, formally trained teachers take to the new role when they can see with their own eyes that the result is not chaos.

These methods mean more work for the teacher, not less. In informal conditions, it is essential for the teacher to keep detailed and accurate accounts of what a child is learning, even though at any given moment she might not know what he's up to. Children help by keeping their own records: in some schools they have private shelves where they store writing books, accounts of experiments and work in "maths," lists of the books they've read, and dates when they checked in with the teacher to read aloud. If American parents could see some of the detailed folders of each child's work, including samples of his art work, they would feel, quite rightly, that a report card is a swindle.

When the class seldom meets as a unit, when children work independently, discipline is less of a problem. It does not disappear as a problem, but it becomes less paramount. The purposeful self-discipline of these children is, we were told, just as surprising to middle-aged Englishmen as it is to Americans. It is a recent development, and by no means the product of luck; much hard work and thought go into the arrangement of these classrooms and their materials. When they work at it, teachers find they can make time during the day for children who need it. "I can give all my attention to a child for five minutes, and that's worth more to him than being part of a sea of faces all day," said a teacher in an East London school overlooking the docks. Other teachers say they can watch children as they work and ask them questions; there is a better chance of finding out what children really understand.

What we saw is no statistical sample. The practices of the good schools we visited in different kinds of communities are not standard, but there are reasons for thinking they are no longer strikingly exceptional. For the most part, these schools are staffed by ordinary teachers from the same sort of background as American teachers; they are not isolated experiments run by cranks or geniuses. The Plowden Committee's massive, and to American eyes, radical report in 1967 indicated that about one-third of England's 23,000 primary schools had been deeply influenced by the new ideas and methods, that another third were stirring under their impact, and that the remaining third were still teaching along the formal lines of British schools in the thirties, and of American schools today.

The change is most widespread and impressive in the infant schools, and becomes more scattered on the junior level. Yet junior schools in some authorities are playing stunning variations on the free themes developed by the infant schools, and these I shall discuss later; but, in general, change in the junior schools is slower, more diffident and complex.

Many formal schools—English and American—are probably doing a more effective job, in conventional terms, than these schools. It doesn't do to dogmatize. For example, by and large, in terms of measurable achievement on conventional tests, children in traditional, formal classes in England do slightly better than children from the freer classes. In one survey cited in the Plowden Report the difference is greatest in mechanical arithmetic, the least in reading. These are facts, but there are reasons for discounting them apart from evidence that the differences disappear in later school years. Formal schools teach children to take conventional tests; that is their function, and it would be surprising if all their efforts didn't produce some results. In view of the lack of test training in the freer schools, the students' results seem to me surprisingly high. The mathematics taught in the informal schools (mathematical relationships in which process of thought counts for more than arithmetical skill) and the English (free writing, rather than grammar and so on) put their students at a disadvantage on achievement tests, whose authors would probably be the first to admit this. England and America badly need new kinds of tests. My own strong impression is that in areas easy to define and probably not hard to test—ability to write, for example, or understanding of the math they were doing—the children in the good schools I saw, including slum schools, were far ahead of students in good formal schools in the United States.

The external motions teachers go through in the schools matter less than what the teachers are and what they think. An organizational change—the free day, for example, or simply rearranging classroom space—is unlikely to make much difference unless teachers are really prepared to act on the belief that in a rich environment young children can learn a great deal by themselves and that most often their own choices reflect their needs. When you see schools where teachers are acting on these assumptions, it is easy to share the Plowden Report's enthusiasm for informal, individual learning in the early years. The infant schools are a historical accident—nobody years ago gave much thought to why children should begin school at five—but British teachers are now realizing their advantages. With kindergarten and the first few years of school fused, children have an extended time in which to learn to read and write and work with numbers. This is especially effective if the pattern of learning is largely individual, if the teacher is important but doesn't stand in the way or try to take over the whole job. Many of the difficulties that plague formal first-grade classes disappear; children aren't kept back from learning, nor are they branded as problems if they take their time.

"Maths"

The Plowden Committee is in a sense the official voice of the primary school revolution in Britain. Its report is, in addition, a complicated document in social history, and to try and draw one single lesson from it would be a mistake. Some of its surveys are of universal interest—one careful study suggests convincingly what common sense has often suggested before, that parents' attitudes play a larger role in a child's life than anything the school does on its own. Some of its chapters are items of political controversy: its excellent proposals for nursery schools and aid to poor areas, for example, have little immediate hope of being pushed through. Some are of purely British interest—the earnest and troubled discussion of compulsory religious education, for example. But an American may be pardoned if one aspect of the report fixes his attention: the extent to which this official document is a radical, if stately, hymn of praise to informal classrooms.

Until fairly recently, heads of many schools could point to a chart in their office showing what each class was doing every minute of the week, and the number of minutes spent on each subject (English, for example, being divided up into periods for spelling, grammar, exercises, composition, recitation, reading, handwriting). It is obvious, as the Plowden Report tartly points out, "that this arrangement was not suited to what was known of the nature of children, of the classification of subject matter, or the art of teaching." Since procedures always affect substance, it is hard to believe that the learning in such classrooms was very much different from that epitomized in a nineteenth-century "Simple Catechism of the History of England Adapted to the Capacities of Young Children," which went like this:

Q: Which was the next king?
A: John, the brother of Richard, succeeded.
Q: What sort of king was he?
A: A very wicked, deceitful, cruel king.

How did change come about? In the first place, a tradition has developed over the last fifty years that gives heads of British schools great freedom in matters of scheduling and curriculum, and teachers a fair amount of say about what goes on in the classroom. By itself this freedom did not produce much change, it is important to note, but it was a prerequisite for reform. Also British schools traditionally have felt relatively free from public and parental opinion. This independence is not a prerequisite to reform, since parents seem to approve the new methods when they understand them; but it is true that people in British schools are not running scared, like their American counterparts who often see public opinion not as a source of policy but as a shadowy, yet massive, veto on all innovation.

Plainly, the infant schools, being distinct institutions, have been able to create separate, more experimental, traditions than schools higher up the educational ladder. They benefited by having to face five-year-olds, for very small children are insistently individual and difficult to herd around. This, and the fact that nursery and infant teachers were often trained together in the same institutions, meant that British teachers were inclined as a practical matter to relate their teaching to basic theories of child development. The characteristic innovations of the primary school revolution were first worked out by a number of infant schools much influenced by practices in progressive nursery schools, whose teachers, in turn, had been absorbing the ideas of thinkers like Montessori, Susan Isaacs, Dewey, and Piaget.

Another element in the reform was a changed emphasis in the work of government inspectors, Her Majesty's Inspectors. As long as the inspectors acted as educational policemen, making the schools toe the mark, their effect over the years was to dampen innovation. But as their role took on more and more of an advisory character they became important agents for disseminating new ideas. There is a moral here: external rules enforced from without not only have little positive effect on schools but tend to make their practices rigidify through fear. Where government and local inspectors have ceased inspecting and taken up advising, the results have been excellent. Some of the lively authorities, such as Leicestershire, have set up distinct advisory offices with no administrative responsibilities except to spread ideas and train teachers in new methods.

The shadow of IQ and achievement tests lay heavy on British schools until recently, and reform has been linked to a partial lifting of that shadow. The pressure has eased most in the few authorities that have successfully abolished the "eleven-plus" examination which used to separate English children at the age of eleven into goats and sheep: a small number of goats went to a "grammar school" that prepared them for a university, while the large number of sheep were sent to a "secondary modern school" that frequently prepared them for nothing. A few secondary moderns are very good indeed, but all too many are simply custodial institutions, like American slum high schools, with the difference that they speak to students in the very English accents of Charles Dickens's Mr. Dombey: "I am far from being friendly to what is called by persons of leveling sentiments, general education. But it is necessary that the inferior classes should continue to be taught to know their position and to conduct themselves properly. So far, I approve of schools." Grammar schools, on the other hand, have traditionally been obsessed with the highly competitive tests for university placement, and therefore, like many crack American high schools, their patterns of instruction are very brittle. ("This is a rat race and I am a rat," as a friend of mine who went to Philadelphia's Central High School put it.) Most British educators are ready now to admit that the eleven-plus was fearfully wasteful of talent and that a test at that age is not a sound prediction of a child's future—except that it becomes a self-fulfilling prophecy with children defined as stupid coming to act stupid. But while the eleven-plus is disappearing, no one is sure what is to replace it.

Authorities are setting up comprehensive high schools, but it is far from certain that Britain will succeed in altering its wasteful, meritocratic patterns of secondary and university education. All this, of course, has a profound if indirect influence on further prospects for change in the primary schools. It is worth emphasizing that the authorities that are establishing alternatives to a system dominated by IQ and achievement tests are also those where reform has moved farthest, even into the junior schools. The moral for reformers on both sides of the Atlantic is, again, obvious. But the problem of tests is a reminder that, dimly, the ultimate fate of the primary school revolution is related to Britain's "long revolution" toward a more equal society; in this limited sense, its aims parallel some of the contradictory social goals of that ambiguous movement in American history known as progressive education.

As in America, there has been a great deal of curriculum reform in England, and this has played a large part in the change. Projects sponsored by the Nuffield Foundation and the Schools Council (a large body composed of representatives of universities and educational organizations, with a guaranteed majority of teachers) are extremely significant, particularly in mathematics, a subject that has undergone dramatic transformation in the last six or seven years. How math is taught illustrates the fusion of classroom practice with new ideas on child development that is characteristic of the new primary school revolution, and I want to go into this important matter in some detail.

Developmental psychology—the study of the growth of intellect and the order in which various abilities flower—has a strong influence on the British schools, but the influence is of a special sort. The same theorists, Baldwin, Isaacs, Bruner, and especially the Swiss psychologist, Jean Piaget, are read in America (along with the dominant American behaviorist school), but to less practical effect. As a rule, theorists have less impact on schools than most people suppose—schools, like girls, are seldom ruined by books—and when they do have an impact, it is usually because their theories confirm successful or popular practices. This is generally the case in Britain today, except that the work of the developmental psychologists, and Piaget in particular, has proved so fruitful and suggestive in the area of mathematics that their assumptions are beginning to pervade

classrooms and shape the direction of educational innovation.

   Among their more important assumptions are that a
great majority of primary school children can't just be told
things, that they learn basic mathematical concepts much
more slowly than adults realize, and that the patterns of
abstract thought used in mathematics ought to be built up
from layer after layer of direct experience—seeing, hearing,
feeling, smelling. According to Piaget, each of us needs to
forge, through direct experience, a mental scheme of the
world, with a hierarchy of meanings; a learner has to organize material and his own behavior, adapting and being
adapted in the process. He learns by his own activity. In a
lifetime's work with young children, including his own,
Piaget has advanced the idea that children learn to think in
stages, and that in the early stages they learn mainly from
the testimony of their senses, and not so much through
words. At first, small children think intuitively and even
magically; at another stage they can deal practically with
concrete experiences; and still later they can think abstractly and make use of mathematical abstractions. In a series of
classic experiments, Piaget offered persuasive evidence that
ideas which seem obvious to an adult are by no means
obvious to a small child. Certain mathematical principles
are difficult to grasp, except through repeated experience.
Take the principle of invariance of number, for example: if
you rearrange five pebbles there are still five. It seems hard
for children to grasp that. Or reversibility: if you reverse a
process—take two beads from eight, then return them—you
arrive at the same state of affairs from which you began.
Of the principle of conservation: if you put a given amount
of water in a flat saucer and pour the contents of the
saucer into a tall glass, many children will say that the

amount of liquid has changed, and it takes both time and experience for them to see that the amount is the same. All this has practical consequences for teaching mathematics: it is of little use to a boy if he can do sums in a workbook but still fails to understand reversal or conservation.

How does a child learn conservation? Much learning involves what often looks to an adult like mere play or mindless repetition. A teacher can quicken learning and direct it along more methodical lines by providing suitable experiences and discussion, but children need time and often learn most efficiently on their own. Conversation is important, and part of the teacher's role with small children is to provide words and phrases when needed. Children are encouraged to talk in the good British primary schools, because, among other reasons, it seems that they make better intellectual progress when they can speak freely about what they're doing and when the teacher is ready from time to time with questions and appropriate terms.

Piaget himself has spelled out a fairly exact sequence of development, from intuitive thinking to being able to reason concretely to the use of abstractions. He has assigned these stages to definite chronological ages. Some teachers question any scheme that pretends to be able to predict what a six- or a seven-year-old can learn, just as some critics have argued that Piaget pays too little attention to the social context of learning—the child's feelings, the expectations of the teacher, and more important, those of the parents. And yet the experience of teachers with mathematics has led to a growing respect for Piaget's general outline of the stages of a child's development. Whether or not his theories are ultimately accepted as true, he and other developmental theorists have pushed British schools in directions that are pedagogically sound, toward an understanding that abstract concepts and words are hard for chil-

dren, that children learn best from their own activity, and
that they need time in which to grow.

Hence the belief of the good infant schools that what
adults call play is a principal means of learning in childhood, a belief that seems more plausible when you consider
how much children learn without formal instruction in the
years before they come to school. Hence the sand and water
tables, the variety of number apparatus, the clay, the wood,
the geometric shapes to arrange, the weights and balances,
the Wendy House, and the dress-up clothes (to explore
adult roles, as well as the materials that make up the
world). Hence, too, the conviction that a classroom should
offer myriads of activities to choose from, that allowing
children to repeat activities is often good, and that language
and experience should link together in conversations among
children and with the teacher.

The Schools Council's admirable *Mathematics in the
Primary Schools* has a handy checklist of the areas of mathematical knowledge of an ordinary seven-year-old by the
time he leaves a good infant school. The list is accurate,
and I'm going to restate some of the main categories and
describe some of the classroom activities related to each.
Remember that in many schools there is no timetable and
no division of the curriculum into separate subjects, so
"maths" will be going on in the classroom at the same time
as painting or reading or writing—much writing, in fact,
consists of accounts of things done in math.

An ordinary seven-year-old knows:

1. Sorting and classifying things into sets (a set is any
defined group of objects); comparing the sizes of two sets,
the number of objects in each; the use of terms for expressing inequalities, more than, smaller than, and so on. As
soon as they come to school, children begin sorting out all
manner of things around the classroom, from buttons to

pieces of material to building blocks. Sorting out merchandise in the play store is one way to learn about sets, as is laying the dinner table in the Wendy House, making sure to get the right number of forks and knives. On their own, small children sort endlessly, like monks at their beads, "four of these, and five of these."

2. Counting; conservation of number; the composition of numbers up to 20—how a number like 7 can be made up of smaller numbers added together (4 plus 3); knowing the numbers up to 20 well enough to see that 14 and 6 are 20 without having to count on fingers. Just as children in these classes learn to write by writing, not by filling in blanks in workbooks, they learn counting by counting. They roam around the classroom making inventories of other children, windows, shoes, chairs, always writing the numbers down. As in reading, they get unfamiliar numbers from each other or the teacher. "Twenty-seven is on the calendar," a boy advises a perplexed little girl who has just finished a count of some milk bottles. They weigh things on scales and balances endlessly: "How many bolts balance nine beans?" Here again the play shop is useful.

3. Knowing the number line—all the numbers in order up to 100; understanding place value in number notation—the fact that each of the 4s in 444 has a value that depends on its place. Many classes have actual number lines, homemade strips of paper a few inches wide and 100 inches long, with the numbers written one per inch in sequence from one to 100, and with the 10s marked prominently with colored magic marker. Along with the big one come number strips of different sizes from one to 10 inches in length; these are used with the big number line to find answers to various problems—addition, subtraction, multiplication. Just by playing with the number line, children can begin to see patterns: if you add 10 to 7 and then keep

going, you begin to sense regularities, 17, 27, 37, and so on.

4. Measurement; rulers and other measuring instruments, including units of money; conservation of measures, liquid and dry (a quart is a quart, whatever the shape of its container); knowledge of the relationship between one unit and another—inches to feet, for example. They invent their own units—their hands, their feet. Children measure the classroom, the playground and everything within. They measure each other, making graphs of heights. They play games guessing the measurement of something and then finding out who guessed best and writing an account to explain why.

5. Simple fraction. The children learn these by dividing up all kinds of real things into halves, quarters, and three-quarters.

6. Aspects of addition, multiplication, and division as these arise from real situations in the classroom. The idea is to have all the first steps performed on real materials, not as abstract exercises. Before a child tackles two times seven, he handles two sets of seven things, and seven sets of two things, using different kinds of objects.

7. Shape and size, including some simple proportions —such as four times as heavy as, twice as tall as, nearly as old as. Children play with shapes, making and copying patterns. Cardboard boxes are cut out, flattened and then rebuilt, the children slowly acquiring a sense of what a cube is; here, work with shapes touches on solid geometry. At one school in Bristol, children noticed that the wooden floor of the assembly hall consisted of squares about a foot on a side, and on a teacher's suggestion, with the help of some fifty-foot lengths of rope, they worked out a game. Following the squares on the floor, pairs of children made polygons with their rope; some were simply large rec-

tangles, most were intricate, with many sides. Then each child would find the area of his polygon by counting (hopping from square to square) the number of squares inside the perimeter. If each child in a pair got a different answer, they recounted. As soon as they were satisfied of the area, the children would begin setting themselves problems to do: for instance, given the fixed length of rope, could you make a figure that had an area of only twenty five squares? Or, after making a shape you liked, how could you modify it to increase the area two squares? The teacher walked around the hall, asking further questions, helping out the children who still had trouble with the basic area of their first figure, and posing new kinds of problems: you might be asked to describe your shape in words alone, without using physical gestures.

An American visitor is impressed not so much by the amount learned—though that is staggering—as by its fundamental nature. What the children know, they know for sure; they have time in which to establish an understanding of extremely basic things that are seldom even taught in American classrooms. First-grade teachers in the United States are sometimes astonished when they discover that many of the children successfully solving workbook sums have no appreciation of, say, the conservation of number; too many children in American schools are taught to memorize multiplication tables without ever having had a chance to understand what multiplication means, and what number relationships are involved.

The approach is mathematical—learning to think— rather than arithmetical, mechanical computation. Rote learning and memorizing have been abandoned by good British primary schools, partly because they bore children and teachers, but more because they are poor ways to learn. It is assumed as a matter of course that each child

will proceed at a different pace, doing different things. The
idea of readiness is seldom used as a justification for hold-
ing a child back—a sure sign that Piaget's influence has been
creative, rather than restrictive, since his theories could
easily be misused. The results in measurable or in less tangible terms are striking. By giving children an opportunity
to explore and experiment—play if you will—and by putting
teachers in a position where they can watch children and
talk to them about what puzzles or intrigues them, good
British schools are producing classes where mathematics is a
pleasure, and where, each year, there are fewer and fewer
mathematical illiterates.

Mathematics illustrates the fusion of developmental
psychology with actual classroom practice, but it is also
becoming in itself an important catalyst for schools making
the change from formal to informal methods of learning.
This is in some part owing to the efforts of the Nuffield
Foundation and the Schools Council. Their curriculum
materials for primary schools are not textbooks or set
courses but rather practical handbooks of suggestions for
teachers in which a large amount of space is given over to
actual samples and pictures of children's work. (The Nuffield math books are dedicated to Piaget.) In sharp contrast
to America, where many of the good curriculum projects
are the work of university people, Britain has taken enormous pains to enlist ordinary primary school teachers in
the process of creating and spreading new ideas and materials.

Teaching Children to Think

Discontented people in Britain sometimes make
polemical use of an imaginary land called America, where
everything is democratic and efficient. My purpose is not to

create another, equally useless myth for the comfort of disheartened American educators. There is nothing utopian about the good British schools I am describing. Teachers are, by American standards, underpaid (salaries start at $30 a week). The turnover in staff is rapid, and schools receive pittances for buying equipment and books. Teaching is often a flat business and always a tough one. It is of immense practical significance that in the flat, tough world of overworked teachers and daily routines, substantial numbers of British primary teachers are organizing their classrooms in a way that really does promote individual learning, that allows children to develop at their own pace in the early years of school.

As examples of this kind of approach, I've described how children learn to read and write, and the careful way in which they are introduced to mathematics. These methods are not guaranteed to make bad teachers, or people who dislike children, into good teachers. But they are more suited than formal methods to the nature of small children and to the kinds of subjects that should be taught in primary school; and they encourage many ordinary teachers, who find that they are happier using them and less likely to spend all their time worrying about discipline. Such methods assume that children can respond to courteous treatment by adults, and that to a great extent they can be trained to take the initiative in learning—if choices are real, and if a rich variety of material is offered them. As the Plowden Report concedes, these assumptions are not true for all children (some will probably always benefit more from formal teaching) or for every child all of the time. But the Report is itself testimony to a growing conviction in Britain that these assumptions can provide a workable basis for an entire nation's schools.

Are they a workable basis for American schools? The

task of creating American schools along these lines will be formidable, to say the very least. This isn't the place to rehearse the institutional and cultural obstacles to change in American education, but I want to anticipate some of the most serious questions that may be raised about the kinds of schools I've talked about. In reform, as in anything else, there must be priorities, and the first priority is simply to see clearly.

Some Americans acknowledge that good British schools are doing better work than good American schools, but they are reluctant to admit that this is because, among other things, children are given freedom to choose from among selected activities in the classroom and to move around the room talking to each other. If they are teachers, they may react to such a proposition with contempt, because they know how hard it is to maintain classroom discipline. Where the class is taught as a unit, and every child is supposed to pay attention as the teacher talks, discipline can be a serious matter; it is even more so when the class splits into groups for reading aloud, as any first-grade teacher knows. Quick children get restless; slow children dread the ordeal, and act accordingly. Any teacher who can keep order under the circumstances has a certain amount of talent, however wasted. Tony Kallet, a perceptive American who worked as an advisor in Leicestershire, has written of the difficulties in maintaining control of the class in the good, but very formal, American school in which he apprenticed. Some children managed quite well, he recalls, but others, especially the "problem children," found the discipline too much, too little was permitted them, and "their problems were, in part, being created, rather than mitigated by control." After working with English classes, he saw matters in a different light, but, for all the time he was in an American classroom, "it did truly seem that every single control imposed was necessary if anything was to be accomplished," a view with which many American teachers will sympathize.

Watching children in British classes working diligently on their own prompts another question: are British children fundamentally different from Americans, and are there critical differences in national character? No doubt there are differences; and yet middle-aged English visitors to the informal schools often react with the same disbelief as American visitors; they find it hard to credit British children with so much initiative and so much responsibility. Also, formal schools in Britain have many discipline problems. American teachers working on their own—and how lonely they seem —have succeeded with approaches similar to those of good British primary schools. Herbert Kohl ran a sixth-grade class in Harlem along fairly free lines and his book, *36 Children*, includes extraordinarily powerful samples of the children's free writing. A British teacher from one of the good local authorities came to a large American city to teach a demonstration class of eight- to eleven-year-olds in a slum school. Before leaving England, he was assured—by Americans—that he would find American children as different from British as day is from night. Yet, the American children reacted exactly as English children to a classroom thoughtfully laid out to permit choices. At first they couldn't believe he meant what he said. After a timid start, they began rushing around the room, trying to sample everything fast, as though time were going to run out on them. Then they "settled remarkably quickly to study in more depth and to explore their environment with interest and enthusiasm." The teacher noticed that for the first two weeks no one did any written English or math, and when he asked them why, they said they hated those subjects. Eventually, he got more and more of the class interested in

free writing, but he never could get them interested in
mathematics. The schools had permanently soured them on
math.

Another argument one hears against this kind of education is that it won't prepare children for life. The answer
the Plowden Report makes to this seems to me sensible:
the best preparation for life is to live fully as a child.
Sometimes this fear takes the reasonable form of a parent's
question: will these informal methods handicap a child if
he moves on to a school run on formal lines? It is a real
question in Britain as children move from good infant
schools to old-fashioned junior schools, or from informal
primary school to rigid secondary school. I went to a parents' meeting at one superb infant school; the parents were
completely won over by the methods of the school, but
they were nonetheless apprehensive of what could become
of their children in a new situation. The head of the school
said that the children did in fact do well in the formal
junior school, which was true. There was only one repeated
complaint about them: they were not very good at sitting
still for long periods of time. In general, an ability to write
and to understand mathematics—to say nothing of an ability to work on their own—stand children in good stead,
whatever school they later attend. Heads of good schools
insist that children are more adaptable than most parents
imagine—and one indication that the problem of switching
from one school to another is not crucial is that most
principals in good local authorities agree with the Plowden
Report's recommendation for another year of the informal
methods of infant school: with an extra year, most of them
think, they could lick their remaining reading problems,
and the transition will be even easier.

Another pressing question Americans ask is, oddly
enough, historical. It is said that these kinds of classes were

tried in the progressive era of American education, and
found wanting. This is one of those historical lessons we
cling to, and, since nothing is as treacherous as our sense of
recent history, it bears looking into. Progressive education,
like the progressive movements in thought and politics, was
woven from many different, often contradictory threads. It
evolved against a background of the great shift in the function of American secondary schools, a change from elite
preparatory institutions to mass terminal institutions; just
as in the 1950s, when our present picture of progressive
education was firmly etched in the popular mind, many
high schools were turning into mass college preparatory institutions. The radical attempt to give secondary education
to the whole American population was an important aspect
of progressive education, just as the reaction against it was
appropriate to an era when nearly half the students in secondary school would go on to college.

As a movement, progressive education reflected a new
concern for science brought to bear on society. In the
schools this meant educational psychology, tests, and the
cult of research. Another element was a concern with social
reform: John Dewey's vain hope that the schools could in
some way become centers for the continuous reconstruc-
tion of society. A distinct, if sometimes related strand, was
an emphasis on individual growth and development. This
last, in particular, was reflected in the practices of a number of American private schools in the 1920s and 1930s.
Good and bad, these schools tended to see children through
ideological lenses: they were followers of Freud, at least to
the extent that they thought repression wicked, and some
idealized children as participants in the artist's historic
struggle against bourgeois society. The best of the "child-
centered" private schools based much of their teaching on
the idea that children come to understand the world

through active play; they tried to get students to take part in the running of the school; they broke down barriers dividing one subject from another, often making the surrounding community and its life part of the school curriculum. These seem today the sounder aspects of their work. The ideological emphasis on liberating the child now appears less useful. In some progressive schools, the energies of staff and children were wasted in testing the limits of permissible behavior, a procedure that was almost forced on the children by an abdication of adult authority. It is not strange that this abdication did not always lead to more freedom: in practice, freeing children from adult authority can mean exposing them to the tyranny of their peers; eliminating "external" rules can mean setting up subtle and unacknowledged rules that are just as ruthless and, even worse, vague and arbitrary.

There isn't much evidence that the classroom practices of the progressive private schools which stressed individual growth ever spread far and wide. The emphasis on cooperation and adjustment to the group was shared by the public school, but it took a different turn: preaching adjustment and "Americanization," the public schools were playing one of their traditional roles—taming objectionable outsiders, shaping them to fit into society, making sure that immigrants and lower class people made the minimum of trouble. The public school wing of the progressive movement in education was thus deeply conservative; obsessed with reform of school administration, putting the operations of the schools more in line with the principles of scientific management espoused by Frederick Taylor and his disciples. (It says much about a misunderstood period that the idea of a school managed as a business was more powerful than the idea of the school as a model civic community, though of course social science, civics, and other shattered fragments of John Dewey's dream did enter the curriculum for better or worse.)

With certain notable exceptions, what we call progressive education was seldom tried in American public schools. In practice, progressive education in public schools meant secondary education for all, and, perhaps, more educational opportunity; more courses, especially in high school, of the life-adjustment variety; more time given to extracurricular activities; more grouping by ability; more emphasis on testing; some "project work" that was no doubt a welcome relief from the textbooks; some more or less important changes in the textbooks themselves; professionalization; new degrees and credentials for educators; and reform in the management of the schools, often based on inappropriate models from the world of business.

What wisps of the vision of education as individual growth trailed into the public schools were largely rhetorical. In their famous study of "Middletown" (Muncie, Indiana) in 1925, Robert and Helen Lynd described the classroom: "Immoveable seats in orderly rows fix the sphere of activity to each child. For all from the timid six-year-old . . . to the . . . high school senior . . . the general routine is much the same." When they returned to Middletown ten years later, "progressive education" had arrived. There was talk of growth, personality development, and creative self-expression: ". . . the aim of education should be to enable every child to become a useful citizen, to develop his individual powers to the fullest extent of which he is capable, while at the same time engaged in useful and lifelike activities." Along with the new rhetoric, the Lynds noted, went increased stress on administration. There was no basic change in methods of teaching or classroom organization. Their report can stand as a paradigm of what progressive education amounted to in most American schools. Education that treats people as individuals had become a cliché without ever being reality.

There are parallels here with the primary school revolution in Britain. It, too, is distantly tied to the changing role of the secondary schools, and certainly much of its rhetoric is reminiscent of our progressive-education movement. British schools certainly share the concern with individual development of the good American progressive schools. And yet the differences in the two movements are profound. Although the British schools stress cooperation, and children are encouraged to teach each other, there is no abdication of adult authority and no belief that this would be desirable. The role of the teacher as active catalyst and stage manager is central. The idea of giving children choices is a considered judgment as to how they best learn. The teaching of mathematics, as described, illustrates how intent these schools are on teaching children to think; they have no particular ideological interest in turning children into social saviours or artistic rebels against bourgeois conventions, or whatever. It is this deep pedagogical seriousness, the attention paid to learning in the classroom, that makes the British primary school revolution so different from American progressive education, which was all too often unconcerned with pedagogy.

This pedagogical focus and what it means can be seen in the way informal British schools are solving the problem of grouping children into classes according to abilities—what the British call "streaming," and what we call "tracking." In both countries it is customary for larger schools to track students so that there are A, B, C, and sometimes D or E classes in a supposed order of ability and intelligence. (And within a class there are slow, average, and fast reading groups.) On the whole, teachers in Britain and America favor the practice, and it is easy to see why. When you deal with the class as a unit, when learning is done by groups, it is less grueling if the group is of roughly similar abilities, and, within limits of conventional instruction, tracking does enable children to go at something closer to their own pace. Tracking, or streaming, is a heated subject in Britain, as it is in America. The spread of informal methods of teaching is calling its utility into question, and many of the schools run on freer lines are abandoning the practice. The Plowden Report, which favors "unstreaming," cites a survey of tested differences between formal and informal schools. It suggests that in terms of measurable achievement, children in tracked schools do slightly but not much better than children in informal schools where tracking has been abandoned. There are, as I have mentioned, grounds for discounting this finding: formal schools train children to take achievement tests, whereas informal ones teach more important things, and we have evidence that the differences in test scores wane as the children grow older.

In England, as in America, there are many reasons why a practical alternative to tracking would be desirable. Tracking in a primary school brands certain children as stupid at an early age, with profound and unhappy effects. "I'll never forget the look on the faces of the boys in the lower stream," an East London junior school head told me. His school has successfully abolished the practice, but he is unable to forget the look: "I still see it when my boys in the lower streams of secondary modern school come back to visit." Tracking has an abiding effect on teachers, too: it tempts them to think that a single pattern of instruction can be applied to a whole class, and it increases the odds that they will deal with their children in terms of abstract categories, IQ, racial stereotype, or whatever. In England, as in America, the upper tracks of a school tend to be middle class, which makes the school even more an instrument for reinforcing social inequity. In America, tracking is commonly a means of maintaining racial segregation within a supposedly integrated school.

After watching British classes, another defect of tracking occurs to you: it ignores the extent to which children learn from each other, slow children learning from the quick, and the bright ones, in turn, learning from the role of teacher they must adopt with the slow. This is most evident in the small number of schools that use family, or vertical, grouping where there is not only no grouping by ability, but no grouping by age, and every class is a mixed bag of older and younger children.

Yet it makes little sense to condemn tracking unless teachers can be shown alternatives to formal classroom teaching. This is where the pedagogical bite of the primary school revolution is so impressive. When a British school stops tracking today, it is not simply returning to the past; it is shifting to a different definition of the roles of teacher and student, and setting up a new kind of classroom in which students are trained to work independently. With the blessing of the Plowden Report, fewer and fewer infant schools track, and it is more and more common for junior schools to abandon tracking in the first two years, and in some cases in the third. How far this trend will go depends on the impact the primary school revolution makes on the secondary schools. One survey in the Plowden Report shows that teachers who used to be overwhelmingly in favor of streaming as a general policy for primary schools are coming to approve of unstreaming. The reason, clearly, is that they are beginning to see workable alternatives.

Tracking is regarded as a necessary evil in America, as are IQ and standardized achievement tests, formal class teaching, specified curriculum materials, set hours for set subjects, fixed ages for entering school, being promoted, and so on. Of course, teachers and administrators realize that children's intellectual and emotional growth varies just as widely as their physical growth, yet they seldom feel able to act on their understanding, to treat each child differently. The good British schools raise serious doubts as to whether these evils are in fact necessary. In America, as in England, there is a growing, and on the whole healthy, skepticism about education. People are questioning the standard methods, and they are becoming realistic about the limited extent to which any school can be expected to pick up the marbles for the rest of society. (One interpretation of the Coleman Report would be that it calls into question all our standard techniques of education, in slums as well as suburbs.) No approach to teaching will solve America's historical and social problems, but, as far as education can make a difference, the work of the British schools in many different kinds of communities suggests practical, working models of individual learning. For those who believe that what American education needs is not more of the same, it suggests alternatives.

The forces that might help bring about similar changes in American schools are few. To some extent the best of the American curriculum projects—such as the Educational Development Center—are pushing schools in the right direction. Good, open-ended materials are often in themselves a kind of retraining course for willing teachers, helping them become more confident about trying informal methods. Curriculum materials are by no means being abandoned in the British schools, but they are making different use of them. Curriculum materials must give teachers and students freedom to use them in a variety of ways; the best materials are often simply handbooks and guides to new approaches, rather than set lessons. Good materials become even more important in the later years of school. Geoffrey

Caston, of the Schools Council, worries that the successful methods of the infant schools, where, of course, the curriculum is largely generated by the students' own activities, will prove less successful when widely applied to older children by teachers of varying abilities. This may or may not be true. I saw junior schools where the free methods of the infant schools were being triumphantly vindicated, but I saw others that were very sleepy and could have used the stimulation of good materials. It is unlikely that curriculum projects can make much difference in America until they find a way of engaging ordinary teachers in creating materials. Americans should profit from the British understanding that the valuable and enduring part of curriculum reform is the process of creation and thought; unless you let teachers in on that, the stuff is likely to be dead. The American curriculum projects and some school systems might help set up equivalents to the advisory centers in good British authorities, teams of teachers and others whose only task is to work in the field with classroom teachers, spreading new ideas. Jerrold Zacharias once proposed display centers that would act as supermarkets for teachers interested in new ideas and techniques. (One role of the advisors in England is to take over classes for teachers so they can attend courses and displays.)

Certainly, useful work could be done developing new kinds of tests in the United States. The IQ and standard achievement tests are not the bogies they are made out to be—I suspect that schools use tests as an excuse to keep from having to try out anything new—but the likelihood of change would be increased if their grip on the minds of school administrators and parents could be loosened. Tests that reflect an ability to express oneself in writing or to reason mathematically would be a help: the problem is to persuade Americans to consider the relevance of standards other than the ones now used. Clearly new tests alone won't solve that. Techniques, particularly when devised by outsiders, are never going to be enough.

It is within the schools that change has to come. Yet the prospects are dim. American private schools that once promoted progressive education are now largely formal in their methods; many are test-ridden, catering to parents who want solid evidence that a second-grade performance will lead to Harvard. They invite John Holt's gibe, "A conservative is someone who worships a dead radical." There are American communities in which principals and teachers are confident of their relationship with parents, and in such places, schools could begin to work along individual lines. Good suburban schools, able to withstand the possibility of slightly lower achievement test scores, also exist, but they seem to be getting rarer. Some of the better Headstart programs may influence the schools to make the first few years of learning more flexible, and perhaps some cities where education has reached a crisis point can be prodded into setting up some freer demonstration classes.

A new class of schools in the United States likely to be interested in informal learning are the community schools which are beginning to appear in a few cities. Yet they have the burden of working out another, perhaps more important, educational problem: how to get parents to participate in the life of the school. This is hard enough, without trying simultaneously to change traditional patterns of classroom teaching. Parents in community schools, like parents everywhere when they face schools, lack convincing models of how things could be different, and they are rightly suspicious of theories and experiments.

This is the point: we lack actual classrooms that people can see, that teachers can work in, functioning schools that demonstrate to the public and to educators the kind of learning I have described. These must be institutions that develop and grow over time, not just demonstration classes. (New York City has tried out every good idea in educational history—once.) To make any impact, such schools will have to be very different from the private experiments of the 1920s and 1930s, with their ideological confusions and their indifference to public education. The temptation is to say America needs many such schools, and we do. But a tiny number of infant schools pioneered the changes in Britain. Careful work on a small scale is the way to start a reform worth having, whatever our grandiose educational reformers might say. In the end, you always return to a teacher in a classroom full of children. That is the proper locus of a revolution in the primary schools.

CHAPTER 2

JUNIOR SCHOOLS

Writing Freely

New classroom practices, styles of teaching and learning, are spreading throughout the better infant schools in Britain. But the reform has not stopped there. Attempts are being made to continue this style of education with older children, too, in the junior schools. Good junior schools in a handful of the leading educational authorities are playing dazzling variations of the free themes worked out with younger children, but they are still relatively rare. Why this is so is worth pursuing. I hope I can suggest some useful answers, although I'm not certain I can. Part of what follows will be about the work of exceptional junior schools; some will be about the efforts of ordinary teachers to pursue, not always successfully, a common idea of what good teaching might be.

Let's begin with writing. It is depressing to go from a fine infant school to a mediocre junior school where the children's confidence in themselves crumbles under the weight of anxieties, drills, and the boredom of rote learning. But a growing number of junior schools are encouraging free writing. Able teachers have always set children to writing, and isolated American teachers right this moment are no doubt shutting the classroom door and telling kids to write their heads off. The significance of what is happening in some junior schools is simply that ordinary teachers are becoming convinced that it is important for primary school children to write on subjects of their own choosing. Though in many cases this hasn't carried them very far, I think it suggests a different set of priorities for teaching young children than those that prevail in America and many parts of Britain.

Things have already started at the infant level, of course, where a big part of what we call the reading program is a writing and talking program. Before they can read, the youngest children are dictating captions and stories to teachers, learning to write them, developing a written vocabulary along with the reading vocabulary. This has many advantages: a child is apt to be interested in what he has to say, though primers and beginning books bore him; there is less class or racial bias to his own material, and the vocabulary will be suitable, because it's his own. Beginning writing is an excellent way to get a good background in phonics, as well as to pick up a working vocabulary of sight words. Good infant teachers say that reading and talking are essential to developing writing; that is why, within limits, children are encouraged to talk to each other, and classrooms are filled with all sorts of books, not just textbooks.

When I speak of writing by five- to eight-year-olds, I'm

not talking about great literary efforts. Some write strings of simple sentences that are barely literate, every sentence beginning with *and*, like the first attempts at popular writing in the Middle Ages. Others are astonishingly precocious, using subordinate clauses, vivid images, and fairly intricate constructions. John Blackie, who has done much to promote writing in British schools, collects some examples in his excellent book, *Inside the Primary School.* They are typical of the ordinary classwork I've seen. Thus a six-year-old boy: "We are going to see a film this afternoon. It is about Boys town in India. We have brought some money to see it. I gave Lewis a penny . . ." Or a seven-year old: "Once upon a time there was a little girl Judy who longed for a doll with long hair at Christmas she wolk up and saw a doll just as she wanted with long hair She played with it all day then at night she put in it a shoe box and forgot to take it upstairs with her in the morning . . ." Note how few serious spelling errors there are. What marks the writing in the better infant schools is sincerity and liveliness; the reader is being told something a writer wanted to say.

In the junior school, as in the infant school, much of the early writing is finished the same day or even in the same period as the children start it. (Junior schools are more likely to divide the day into periods.) Gradually the time for writing can be extended. In the junior schools, too, children alternate between small reports on their own experiences—including things they've done in science and math—and stories which may take their themes and heroes from television and adventure stories, and, less often, from fairy tales. Some of the nine-, ten-, and eleven-year-olds are more apt to show literary influences in their writing, picking up the tricks of any writer they happen to be reading. A few children, like literary hacks, get used to standard formulas. For this reason, teachers who are serious about writing try to steer children away from stories of the "Once upon a time . . ." sort, at least at the outset.

Schools that require set subjects and themes tend to get derivative and contrived work. The Plowden Report holds no brief for teachers who force children into "stock phrases and insincerity by setting them to write on the conventional subject: the walk in spring, the autobiography of a penny, the loaf of bread, or the tree, which may culminate in 'I am happy as a table, but I was happiest as a tree.'"

Teachers sensitive to quality try to make sure that writing doesn't become a chore; they are reluctant to push children to write unless they seem genuinely interested. If children are to write freely, many say, it is important to let them choose what can be read aloud, what is only for the eyes of a teacher or a friend, and what is secret, the property of the author. When children grow confident, teachers encourage them to make books with folded pieces of paper and slightly thicker covers. Some classes have a large display rack for these books, which children pick and choose according to their tastes. The books contain personal writing, some poetry (usually unrhymed), stories, accounts of math and science projects, or topics of some sort of another from cavemen to hobbies. Some of the writing derives from information books in the classroom—volumes on birds, ancient Britons, or whatever. Where there is no incentive to copy, children don't. Where there is, they do. Sir Alec Clegg, the chief education officer of the West Riding in Yorkshire, has gathered some work of children in his authority into a fascinating collection called *The Excitement of Writing*.* I wish American school authorities would take a good look at this book. Here's a boy, 10:

*Alec Clegg, *The Excitement of Writing*, London: Chatto and Windus Ltd., 1966. This material is reprinted by permission of the County Council of the West Riding of Yorkshire and Chatto and Windus Ltd.

I can remember that hour I walked on the sands by a very rough sea. The waves crashed down so hard I could feel the trembling of them on me. It sounded like bricks tumbling down from an old house when it is being knocked down. . . .

Here's a girl, 11:

We set out, Mummy and I, we were going into the town. I was delighted, for I was to have a pair of new shoes, they were to be for school. When we got to the town we went into a shoe shop. I saw a few pairs of shoes but I didn't like any of them, the women then brought out another pair of shoes brown and ugly. Mummy liked them. I looked at her in horror unable to speak surely, surely she wouldn't buy them. But the purchase was complete and she had bought them. I pinched myself to make sure it wasn't a dream, unluckily for me it wasn't. . . .

This is a ten-year-old, writing about a candle:

White Polish; sour milk,
Delicate finger wrapped in cotton blanket.
Star growing, bigger, bigger flickering in
    darkness,
A great Lord, now a humble person bowing.
Golden crystals, dark eye,
Slowly, flowing, running milk.
Faint glimmer of hope, trying to enlarge itself.
Black burned pie; all beauty gone.

The writing inevitably reflects teachers' concerns. Some teachers are impresarios, hustling formidable feats of child-writing—they inspire you with a self-righteous itch to remind them that the job is to help a kid along and not promote an author. (As Mr. Clegg wisely points out, what gets written in any school is pretty much a by-product, the main point being the development of the child himself.) There are Miss Jean Brodies who encourage marvelous fairy tales, poetry, fantasies, and all kinds of creative writing, but who ignore precise and elegant math and science reporting going on right under their noses. In writing, as in other matters, it is difficult to exaggerate the extent to which schools everywhere are bearers of the genteel culture and its class biases. Still, where local authorities and principals have encouraged free writing, it is impressive to see that many teachers do learn to respect the content of children's writing without being shocked or disapproving or niggling about inessential errors. (The students of emancipated teachers produce writings about sex and life in the raw, some of which are true.)

Writing is getting across what you have to say, and the teachers in the best British classes I visited tried to treat mistakes in grammar, spelling, and messiness as obstacles to communication. They let slips go by without undue comment. Correcting writing is extremely difficult in classes of forty or so, but watching good teachers, you begin to see the priorities: it is easier to help children with language if you have a basis for diagnosing what you need to know. In part, you get the raw material for a diagnosis from writing. You also find out more if the classroom routine is arranged so that you can listen and watch and, at least occasionally, *talk* with a child. A lot of teachers try to correct all mistakes in one-to-one talks with a child. There is no point in scribbling red marks over somebody's personal statement. John Blackie has an ugly story of a nine-year-old whose theme, "My Father," told about his dead parent. The teacher's only written comment was: "Tenses. You keep mixing past and present."

Nowhere is it clearer than in correcting, that a central part of teaching is relationships between people, which are impossible to speak of in a general way. The finest analytical nets will never land a pure example of good teaching, any more than they will deliver up pure specimens of friendship or love. We are condemned to rough impressions, which nearly always float up to the level of platitudes, about as useful as advising people not to take any wooden nickels. Still, for what it's worth, good teachers pay serious attention to the *content*, the subject of the piece of writing (or the painting). There is this bond of interest between them and the children. Children are interested in finding out if a meaning has come across and what the reader feels about it, and many are quite ready to accept criticism. If it's an unfinished story, the teacher inquires how it's going to end. He asks how the child came to choose this subject. He makes an effort to talk thoughtfully about specific details, asking when, how, why. Sometimes he'll want to know if the writer is pleased with his work, and if he answers no, the teacher might wonder if he doesn't have some ideas on how it could be better. All the rules of thumb fall away before the rule that says the worst thing is to discourage future work. There is never enough teaching to go around. Teachers try to enlist the children to do some of the correcting—many ask the class to spot errors in the books or other writings on display in the room and bring them to the attention of the author, who can then make the corrections himself.

The work of good junior schools runs increasingly against the grain of the British educational system as the children get older. Even in very free junior schools, a visitor sometimes notices a decline of the superb work of the first few years as children are tuned up for examinations. Competition for university places is keen, and a child's fate still rests largely on getting into the right secondary school. This is not the whole story, and I'll return to the point later; what I want to point out now is the way in which what is taught comes more and more to resemble the standard fare in American schools. There are plenty of exceptions— enough to make me doubt that the process is inevitable; most of the exceptions are in authorities where free methods have become a reigning orthodoxy. Still, it is depressing to see good junior schools succumbing to the idea that there is a separate subject called English, and giving the children spelling lists, workbooks, and grammar exercises, as though anybody ever learned much that way. In a school where children's writing is well supervised there is no place for grammar and spelling as distinct subjects. It is absurd to think that if a child can take somebody else's sentences to pieces and label the parts he will write better ones of his own. Correctness comes from using the language and hearing it used under sound guidance. People learn to write correctly by writing, not by plowing through mountains of workbooks.

There is no general formula that fits all schools that encourage good writing. Mr. Clegg makes a stab in the right direction when he says that they respect children, and that they are more concerned with how they learn than what they learn. The same attitude that led them to encourage free writing led them to stop grouping classes by ability. First-hand experience stimulates good written work; and for at least part of the day in most of the schools, children are given choices about what to do.

I grant that this is all vague. So is what the teachers presiding over the best classes told me. They all said that children write for people they trust, that they don't write freely until they can talk with confidence, and that except for the work of certain born storytellers most of their best writing comes from things they experience directly. There is no getting around it; if we want the kind of schools where children write freely—which is not something separate, but only an emblem, after all, for a whole way of teaching—we had better understand that there simply are no shortcuts.

Math and Art

Like good infant schools, the best junior schools resist compartmentalizing the school day into separate periods of separate subjects. This is important to keep in mind in what follows, which is a description of math work with older children. As with writing, good math instruction does not necessarily have to take place in math periods; it may be connected with what we would call science instruction or art or "English." Mathematics is still the wasteland of the primary school curriculum in England, as in America; I don't wish to exaggerate the good news. My only claim is that some of the British experiences with junior children in math can help us as we alter our notion of what a good school looks like.

In talking about math in infant schools, I mentioned the fusion of developmental psychology, and particularly the work of Piaget, with classroom practice. Many teachers are starting to base their teaching on the idea that most young children learn best through using concrete materials, and that a basic understanding of mathematical concepts ought to come through children's own activities in classrooms designed for permitting choices. It seems axiomatic to good infant teachers that children learn at different paces and in different ways, and that simply telling them things or setting them to do workbook sums is a poor way to introduce them to mathematical reasoning. The teacher is there to provide the kind of experiences that will help childen along in their thinking; an essential aspect of such experiences is conversation among kids, as well as between teacher and pupils. The aim is to acquire a basic understanding of numbers and their relationships—mathematics, not Victorian arithmetic.

There are extremely formal junior schools in Britain where mathematics is taught informally—where the authorities have looked at the results of the new curriculum materials and found them good—but in other schools math work has become a step toward a whole new curriculum, the kind of free or integrated school day that many infant schools have had for years. (These terms, like most educational slogans, quickly become an embarrassment.) Where teachers are interested in escaping the tyranny of timetables and the various iron and bamboo curtains separating primary school subjects, math is serving as a focus for reform. The introduction of homemade and commercial math apparatus into dreary junior classrooms has helped reassure teachers that older children, too, will learn through their own activities, encouraging teachers normally uncomfortable with math—which means most primary school teachers—to think in new ways about numbers. The apparatus and the new curriculum materials are important, but my impression is that the various new materials are more significant for teachers than for children. Teachers who have used materials to put themselves in a position where they can watch children working and help their learning have taken the first steps toward a different way of teaching. A "maths" class where this kind of change is happening is an exciting place to be: work starts spilling over into other periods; the teacher finds that it makes sense to let children continue without interruption when they've become absorbed in something—indeed, that this sustained absorption is one of the points of the whole enterprise. They also come to see the benefits to all children of finishing a piece of work to one's satisfaction.

Specifically, this means that textbook problems give way to problems children and teachers devise, not irrelevant situations but real problems—how much water is lost from a leaky hose in the backyard? Most arithmetic books and workbooks present word problems that are mechanical exercises in mufti, involving little thought, simply the mindless application of a formula that many children never understand. By contrast, the Plowden Report cites an example of what can emerge from excited juniors: a group of ten-year-olds had collected a number of bird and animal skulls and wanted to measure the capacities of the brain cavities. They devised a method for measuring them—filling the skull cavities with sand—and then had to make a cubic container for measuring the sand. A cubic inch worked for the cat and rabbit skull, but not for the bird's skull, so they worked out a quarter-inch container. Some adults would see this as a trivial exercise, not really a mathematical problem at all, but children who know that cubic measurements are to be used are way ahead of children whose heads buzz with a mysterious formula like $l \times w \times h$. Few adults would have been able to devise as elegant and simple a solution to a difficult question of measurement.

A central aspect of good math work is figuring out the different ways to communicate results. Much of math is writing, graphing, illustrating, as well as talking. When children show good teachers how they arrived at an answer, a question might be: now think of a different way to do it, and a different way to record the results. Children pick up techniques and symbols as they need them. Sometimes it turns out that what they need is linked to an advanced piece of math that a conventional curriculum would not offer them until secondary school. Well-intentioned British teachers, lacking mathematical confidence, condemn children to the study of the eternally mundane—the postman, numbers in the candy shop—on the assumption that, since children need concrete practice and practical work, they are only interested in the concrete and the everyday. (Something akin to the old progressive notion that the postman or the sanitation board was more suitable for children to study than Renaissance Florence.) Successful teachers find, on the contrary, that children at all stages of development can move on from practical materials to an interest in purely mathematical questions: you see impressive work in algebra and geometry where this approach has flowered.

To carry work through to such a point, teachers need to be thinking mathematically all the time—which is not to say that they need to start as first-rate mathematicians. Many find the plans of work for math in the primary years set out by the better English curriculum projects—and often by their own schools—helpful as bulwarks against their own sense of chaos and confusion. American teachers interested in these sorts of curriculum materials—which are guides for children's work, not potted lessons—should take a look at the Nuffield Foundation math series (published in the United States by John Wiley and Sons) and the Schools Council's *Mathematics in the Primary School*, which is in some respects closer to the actual work going on in the better junior and infant schools. Experienced teachers will find them a challenge, recognizing that they imply a wholly different approach to math. Inexperienced and unsure teachers will find them disturbing, because they call into question many of our standard notions of what teaching is about. In the infant years, numbers and relationships between them are stressed; in the junior years, volume, weight, length, shape, and size, leading children to proportion, symmetry, and certain aspects of geometry, and graphs leading them in some cases to algebra.

On the whole, space is used much less imaginatively in the ordinary junior school than in the infant schools. Teachers groping for an informal approach with juniors are startled to realize that much of that standard classroom baggage is unnecessary. A teacher doesn't need a desk *that* big, and children don't need individual desks if they have proper places to store their things. If stand-and-deliver methods of formal class teaching—the teacher up at the blackboard, chalk in hand, talking at people—are largely abandoned, then it is no longer necessary for everybody to see the blackboard. In schools that have moved toward freer methods, the room is often divided into workshop areas roughly like those of the infant school. Cupboards, bookcases, pegboards, and rolls of corrugated cardboard serve as room dividers, storage places, and display racks. Tall cupboards are ideal as lockers and room dividers. If you don't need desks, you do need lots of flat working surfaces, tables, which some teachers make by putting desks together and fitting old blackboards over them. As in the infant schools, activity flows out into the corridor and out of doors, where there is more work space. Children work alone or in small groups. Some teachers find that pairs of children are an excellent working unit; pairing encourages discussion of how to get and record results. Others prefer working parties of three or four, at least for math. In large classes, most teachers are forced to take some remedial groups of three or four, even though they may not approve of ability grouping. (Most junior schools still group rigidly by ability, though a growing number of teachers look with disfavor on the practice.)

Storage is a problem. Teachers easily come to grief through failing to enlist the children in general housekeeping and management of a classroom. Stuff has to be stored so children can get it and return it themselves, and some of that stuff costs money—quality is important. On the other hand, one good pair of scales is worth five tinny ones. A good microscope is worth fifteen poor ones. You don't need forty sets of everything; but, just for working with measurement and numbers over a few years, a well-stocked school will have Dienes multi-base and algebra material, Cuisenaire rods, Stern appartus, number lines, and all sorts of measuring tools, including tape measures and surveyor's chains, map measures, trundle wheels, large wooden cali-

pers, kitchen timers, stop watches, spring and simple balances, bottles for liquid measures. Much stuff is homemade,
acquired over a long period of time.

Although teachers become dubious about the value of
formal class instruction, in practice they do hold class ses-
sions when there is something for all to hear. If some share
my skepticism about a group of thirty or forty as a learning unit, others say they find themselves coming round full
circle to a certain amount of group discussion on a much
deeper level than the sort of forced discussions that occur
when children don't have any common experiences under
their belt to talk about. This has to be a matter of judgment and temperament.

Good junior school teachers concede that there is a
limit to the extent to which all interesting or useful math
can come from children's activities. In some infant schools
and a few junior schools, it can and does. But the limita-
tions on most schools, teachers, and children usually require compromises. It is hard to work individually with
children in big classes; it is hard for a teacher to find out
what intrigues or puzzles some children unless there is some
way first to involve them in *doing* something, just to get
them started. Thus, as a halfway house to the kind of free
classroom they would like to organize, some teachers begin
with handmade assignment cards suggesting a variety of
math activities to try—things to weigh, rates of speed to
compare, and so on. At first these are made by the teacher,
and usually they are color-coded for different areas of
mathematical understanding—problems about length will be
red, problems of volume, blue. They are put someplace
where kids can get at them, and it is common even in fairly
formal British schools to see pairs of children working
through them on their own. Teachers arrange them in sequences of increasing complexity and difficulty, sometimes

approaching very advanced topics, such as a card I saw that was the first of a series on a pendulum. "Make a pendulum with some plasticene and string and a thumb-tack. Play around with it and record what you notice." Later cards suggest more questions on the rate of swings and what affects the time they take. Imaginative cards end up by asking a child a quite open question, such as whether what he's done related to another card he'd done and how. The best often close with suggestions to make up a problem yourself and write it into the form of an assignment card for others. Children can completely rework and restock a collection of cards, making them much more interesting if a teacher encourages them.

Obviously, the cards can be just as much of a crutch for teachers and children as an ordinary textbook, and I have seen classes use them that way. They are a severely limited art form: simply a way to take some of the burden of teaching a whole class off the teacher, encouraging individual work by the children at their own pace. For teachers who believe in giving a solid background in several definite areas of math, records of which cards a child has worked through pinpoint the areas where more work needs to be done. But the cards can never do more than provide an initial setting, a classroom where children are working with materials and shapes, and where a teacher is free to take his time, watching them messing around and responding to questions. Teachers who use them as a bridge to freer work introduce a set, change the cards as the children use them and develop interests, and then slowly discard them as more and more work comes from children's topics. (I saw very few topics by a whole class that were of the quality of topics done by small groups or individual children.)

Record-keeping is important, although teachers insist that it is not good practice to have children record everything they do. Writing a math "book" or doing a graph is a good idea only if recording results will add to the experience, and not take away from it. In some classes, children keep their own mathematical record books; where assignment cards are used, the children generally check off their own progress on a wall chart. When they need to practice sums or workbook problems, the teacher frequently has them check their own answers. The best sort of teacher's records take two forms: a running log of comments on strengths and weaknesses of individual children and their accomplishments, and individual files of the children's work sampled in some systematic fashion over a period of time.

Although the quality of teaching and children's work varies immensely, what takes place in most infant classrooms is pretty much the same. Not so in good junior classes, where every student is doing something different. So a general checklist of various activities in mathematics conveys very little. A visitor to such classes wants to get beyond surface impressions to discover something of the history, what has been happening to teachers and children, the sequences and rhythms of work over days and weeks. Children aren't bad as sources, but their memory is short, and in any case the subject of their own education leaves them cold. Teachers, for their part, find it hard to reconstruct what goes on over time; they are too immersed in the present. And successful teachers, as the Plowden Report notes, are often the ones least able to articulate what they've been trying to do.

Lacking really good firsthand accounts by teachers (and, ideally, children), we have to settle for fragments and guesses. Some teachers try to alter their teaching in isolation; some are in schools where a principal or a local advisor gives encouragement. Sometimes a teaching principal will take the lead by himself. Many start modestly with a period on, say, Friday afternoon in which the children are free to mess around with practical math. Others begin by getting a group—eight is a common number, for some reason—involved in practical math work each day, while the rest of the class goes about its normal routine. There are various combinations of approaches with assignment cards, practical materials, and, in schools where teaching in other areas is loosening up, other subjects.

One teacher who wrote an account of her class for a curriculum project said she began by deciding to base all teaching on the premise that no child should be asked to accept a mathematical truth on her authority, which meant that she had to arrange matters so children could learn for themselves. To her surprise, she found herself weakest on fundamentals—she easily grasped difficulties in complex situations, but she had never fathomed the depths in apparently simple math questions: "It will be appreciated that after twenty years of teaching mathematics, such an admission was not an easy one to make." She discovered that wherever posssible it was best to use material from the immediate environment: leaves from trees were a better "apparatus" for understanding perimeter and area than rectangles, so her pupils fitted string along the edges of leaves, and got the area by laying the leaves on flat pieces of paper marked off in square units. After a time, she estimated, the children were spending about a third of the time experimenting with materials, a third of the time discussing what they found with each other and the teacher, and a third practicing conventional math skills. She found little difference in this last; their workbook computations were the same as before. They began detailed explorations: "From a study of making polygons rigid, by means of division into triangles, came an interest in bridges and towers; from tessellation with hexagons came an interest in bees, patchwork quilting, and modern architecture; and from a study of volume, and finding the weight of air pressing on the whole human body at various heights, came an interest in mountaineering. . . ."

The mathematical learning I'm describing is not widespread, but it exists. The Plowden Report estimated that somewhere between ten and twenty percent of English primary schools had substantially modified their mathematics teaching in these directions. Many people I talked with would put the estimate much lower, and there is a good deal of concern that the gains that have been made thus far at the junior level will not last.

The arts, too, are serving as an instrument for change in a few junior schools in Britain. Indeed, if the slow and uncertain educational reform has a traceable beginning, it lies in the 1920s and 1930s, when scattered teachers saw the results of encouraging children to paint on huge pieces of paper with real powder paints, not watercolors. A. L. Stone, who retired recently as an advisor in the West Riding, wrote a sketch on art in a slum school where he was principal in the early 1940s. His *Story of a School* is an extremely close and perceptive account of the effect of expressive work in one school.* Its vision of every child as an artist has an old-fashioned, progressive ring, but it speaks for a vital and continuing tradition.

When Stone came to this school in its bleak setting, he managed to convince some of his teachers to concentrate on the arts. He believed that if you could encourage confidence and interest in the arts, other things—including the three Rs—would follow. So the school set about introducing children to unlimited color, all sizes of paper, clay in big hunks, mimes and massed movement, music.

What happened with clay was typical: some children played with it and quickly became surfeited, others went

*A. L. Stone, *Story of A School*, Her Majesty's Stationery Office, 1949.

on to become deeply absorbed. The greater the child's interest, the more self-discipline he would show, and the longer he would be able to concentrate. In the end, Stone found himself gauging the results of teaching by watching the intensity of the child's concentration.

In one class, children began moving and miming history lessons, Romans fighting ancient Britons. There was awkwardness and too much at the outset was done by the teacher, but gradually the children were moving to quite basic themes, working out their own variations on walking, skipping, running, hopping. As they grew more assured, they tried out simple dramas: miming creeping toward a tree, seeing something that scared you, running away. Stone compared a Nativity scene in the first year with another two years later. In the first, much of the liveliness of the drama was killed by practice. In the second, the kings walked to Bethlehem as kings should, regally. There came a stage in the miming when children needed to frame silent speeches to themselves, and short commands and brief monologues grew common. The children sometimes wanted to record a scene that came out particularly well, and they would take great pains with the writing of what eventually became plays.

The first results in painting were pleasant enough, but nothing special. With the development of movement and mime, the children's art work came to life. Stone and his teachers began to suspect that when children were deeply involved, the results would most always be satisfying, and that good work in one area would spill over in countless ways to other subjects. (To Stone's disappointment, however, the work in math and music remained fairly formal and poor.) Stone and his staff saw something of a pattern emerging in art: most children seemed to need a period when they just fooled around, often unproductively as far as any adult eye could tell; then, they explored whatever medium they were working in; and, at some third point, they wanted help in getting something across. It was then that teaching could be most effective. Science teachers like David Hawkins, have also noted this basic pattern.

The most successful teachers in the best schools I visited talked in similar terms about art. Far from being a frill or something to keep the children busy with when they finished their academic chores, art is regarded as essential, a touchstone of good teaching. The most striking difference between the many ordinary and the few excellent junior schools I saw was the vividness and variety of what was done in paint, clay, wood, textiles, linoleum, wood cuts, metals, and prints. Invariably the quality of the art told a great deal about the standards of the school in all areas of the curriculum.

I should add a word about drama and movement. Drama at the infant level starts with improvisations in the classroom touched off by some event, as when kids get caught up in a story. With juniors, it can range from wordless mime to plays that achieve a full written script, generally put on by the children for their own benefit, not for any wider audience.

It's not necessary to have anything beyond space, time, a few all-purpose costumes, and perhaps a percussion instrument or two. With the younger children, teachers start with simple suggestions: pretend the classroom is a jungle or a mountain, or the scene of a historical event. (Some wonderful variations can come from getting children to imagine they're making their way across the bottom of the ocean, and it's fascinating to see the relish very *good* children take in playing a witch, a poisoner, or Herod.)

A lot of what is called movement is hard to categorize. It can be drama, exercise, or something close to dance. (It's always seemed odd to me that modern dance, one of the few distinctively American art forms, has made so little inroad in American schools.) The spread of movement has been paralleled by the development of climbing and other kinds of apparatus for individual work in physical education classes. Movement is a perfect physical metaphor for the type of education I'm talking about, but it's hard to describe. Short of trying out some movement—which can be ludicrous in the hands of an inept teacher—or seeing a class for themselves, the best way for American teachers to get an idea of what it's like would probably be through a film. The Schools Council in Britain is preparing one and an American filmmaker, Henry Felt, also has one in the making.

Why So Few Good Schools?

I've used examples in writing, math, and the arts to show some of the work done in good junior British schools. But why are there so few of them? I can only hazard a few guesses.

The Plowden Report described a survey made some years ago, which said that as children went from the infant to the junior level there is a

> narrowing of opportunities, a tendency toward regimentation, a substitution of group or even class teaching for individual work. Many children tackled less difficult work and wrote less in their own words than they had done some months before. The libraries in the youngest junior classes were often inferior in quality and range to those the children had left behind in the top infant classes, and children spent more time on "readers" and less on real books. Individual interests in music and art and craft had petered out. Some boys whose ability and attendance were average or poor had fallen back in almost every respect when seen four months after transfer. They made little perceptible headway by the end of the year.

This is probably less true today, for more junior schools have altered their ways. Many of the junior schools I saw were at least struggling to change, if not always with great success. But in others, the danger signals the Plowden Report cites in another context were too evident: "Fragmented knowledge, no changes in the past decade, creative work very limited, much time spent on teaching, few questions from the children, too many exercises, too many rules, frequent punishments, and concentration on tests."

One important reason for the rigidities of junior schools is the secondary schools they serve. What is wrong with British secondary schools is a long, long story, but in general they are even more meritocratic than American high schools; they brand more kids as failures; they are as prone to teach a curriculum and set subjects that don't make sense to a lot of their students. What the system does to failures is obvious. It may be even more illuminating to note what it does to successes. Richard Hoggart has described the state of mind of the scholarship student, the product of the upper reaches of the British system. It may have a familiar ring to American readers:

> He begins to see life, for as far as he can envisage it, as a series of hurdle jumps, the hurdles of scholarships which are won by learning how to amass and manipulate the new currency. He tends to over-stress the importance of examinations, of the piling-up of knowledge and of received opinions. He discovers a technique of apparent learning, of the acquiring of facts rather than of the handling and use of facts. He learns how to receive a purely literate education, one using only a small part of his personality and challenging only a limited area of his being. He begins to see life as a ladder, as a permanent examination. . . . He becomes an expert imbiber and doler-out; his competence will vary, but will rarely be accompanied by genuine enthusiasms. He rarely feels the reality of knowledge, of other men's thoughts and imaginings, on his own pulses; he rarely discovers an author for himself and on his own. In this half of his life he

can respond only if there is direct connection with the system of training. He has something of the blinkered pony about him; sometimes he is trained by those who have been through the same regimen, who are hardly unblinkered themselves, and who praise him in the degree to which he takes comfortably to their blinkers .... As a result when he comes to the end of the series of set-pieces, when he is at last put out to raise his eyes to a world of tangible and unaccommodating things, of elusive and disconcerting human beings, he finds himself with little inner momentum. The driving-belt hangs loosely, disconnected from the only machine it has so far served, the examination-passing machine.*

The ethos Hoggart captures so vividly is surely part of the reason why excitement wanes in the later years of school. All schools mirror their social order. All, in addition to teaching rudimentary skills, and passing on certain elements of a common culture, socialize children to adult society and sort them out socio-economically. As the children grow older—as they reach the secondary schools—the curriculum is increasingly narrowly defined, in academic terms, and there is more and more pressure on the schools to serve one particular function: to provide the credentials that justify separating out those who make it from those who don't. This is the great barrier to further reform; it may mark the outer limits of the possibilities of school reform in a fundamentally unequal society. Indeed, the interesting thing about the British example is that they have been able to go as far as they have toward making the early years of schooling decent and humane, despite the overwhelming class biases of the educational system.

The slowness of change in junior schools can also be accounted for by the fact that reform has seeped upward from nursery and infant schools, whose methods were

*Richard Hoggart, *The Uses of Literacy,* London: Chatto and Windus Ltd., New York: Oxford University Press. Reprinted by permission.

worked out over thirty years. There isn't the backlog of traditions and materials that many of the infant schools now have. Older children need a large amount of open-ended curriculum material, too. A lot of junior classrooms look starved for books and stuff.

It may be particularly unlucky that the spread of informal methods from infant to junior schools has been occurring at a time when primary education in Britain is badly understaffed and underfinanced. The cumulative neglect of the primary schools—the Cinderellas of the system—is fascinating and depressing, since they are by far the most creative and important part of British education. In a number of places I visited, a junior school that was accounted pretty good two or three years ago was no longer considered worth looking at. Turnover of staff had completely altered the picture. Arthur Razzell has described how a principal feels who has developed some good teaching only to watch his staff disappear, to be replaced by people who have never worked informally before:

> Either I had to revert to a more formal and directed system of teaching until my colleagues had settled down and were in a position to try out new ways of working, or else I had to plunge straight on, giving all the support I could, and hope that they would be prepared to tackle informal teaching. Whichever course I took it was clear that our experimental work had come to an end too early for us to judge whether it was effective or not.

Thus, many fear that inadequate funds and staff will check the progress of a reform that has made such impressive gains in the infant schools. One or two of the gloomier, older veterans, about to retire, worry that the Plowden Report could become the highwater mark of a progressive movement that is already spent.

Yet the movement seems far from spent in the authorities where change has spread farthest, and where the sort of thing I have been describing is flourishing. I imagine that in Leicestershire and Oxfordshire there will be more and more examples of this kind of teaching—in schools staffed by ordinary teachers. It is especially moving to visit an authority like the West Riding, where, in the face of incredible staffing problems and poverty, reform still spreads. There, harassed school authorities and teachers keep a vision of what good teaching can be. In such areas, it is hard to believe that the secondary schools can remain unchanged against the force of their vision.

It is as a first step toward such a vision that I've tried to give concrete examples, to arrive at some specific notions of what a good job looks like. It seems to me that the time has come to stop endlessly asserting objectives—discipline, the liberal arts, the three Rs, basic education, even freedom and spontaneity—without being specific about how the objectives are reached.

Let me conclude this brief account of some British schools by returning to the specific. Talk of children's writing may seem far-fetched, like giving IBM typewriters to monkeys, until you see schools where children *are* writing. Then a number of things occur to you about what should be going on in schools. Writing is a good way to learn, because an emphasis on written expression makes it more likely that children will build on the mastery of language they already possess, instead of having it destroyed, which is what so many American reading programs end up doing. This is not an argument for a crash program of three hours of writing every morning; writing can't be taught in isolation as a separate subject. There must be something to write about. There have to be books of all sorts available (who wants to write about Dick and Jane?), and there has to be talk.

If many people write most freely about their own experiences, then a priority in organizing the school day becomes providing a setting for experiences out of which writing and other kinds of expression can come. (They can, of course, be vicarious and imaginative experiences in realms far removed from everyday existence.) You can't, in most cases, get writing from children by command, but the more varied things there are to do and to choose from, the greater the likelihood of engaging children with diverse interests. This ought to be the start of a new curriculum.

There is something else about writing. It offers the teacher the possibility of playing a different role from the conventional one. There isn't a correct answer, for one thing. (Not that there's anything wrong with learning that sometimes there is one right answer, but the schools have beaten that point into the ground.) Since the experience is the child's own, he has to stick to it if the writing is to be honest. The teacher can't know more about it than the student; the teacher can be catalyst, editor, audience, guide, drawer-out, but she has to work with what the child gives. The student and teacher can both be—I wouldn't say on equal terms, for that is fairly rare—sharing a concern for the piece of writing and what it says. Thus there is a basis for a conversation, something that is fairly unique in most schools. In a different context, talking about science, David Hawkins has described this as an "I-thou-it" relationship—teacher and student seeing each other in mutual, working relationship to some portion of the world around them, a pendulum, a tube filled with glycerine, soap bubbles, and, I would add, some writing or clay sculpture. Until a child is working on something, a teacher has little to go on. Once there is something both are preoccupied with, the ground is laid for a man-to-man discussion. My impression of one kind of awful classroom reinforces this: far from being impersonal, the room is filled with everybody's consciousness that a scary relationship exists between students and teacher. There is nothing but this relationship, and nothing gets learned. In good classes, relationships between students and teachers grow out of common interests. Cultivating these interests is the job of teaching.

Also, a teacher working with a child on a piece of writing can perform a real service—encouraging expression, helping the child improve. Both the teacher and the child sense this; it colors the relationship. A deep, unstated problem of the schools, a problem that gets worse as children grow older, is that what teachers have to teach is frequently not worth learning. One reason teachers in the early years of school seem happier than most is that they are teaching something that matters, reading. In later years teachers are apt to be shaky about the value of what they're doing, with good reason. In writing, as in other areas, the work of the English schools I've described is focused on things that most teachers and children would consider worth the effort. The contrast with the sludge of memorized trivia in the later years of our primary schools is stunning.

Learning from British Teachers

To what has been said here about British schools, some points of special interest to teachers and administrators may be added:

1. Although I don't wish to present the methods described simply as a better way to learn the three Rs, I do want to note that there are few reading problems in good British schools; and heads of schools predict that the few remaining problems will diminish when the informal methods of the infant schools are extended for another year.

2. British teachers, like teachers everywhere, pray for small classes, but informal methods work in classes of forty children. It would clearly be better for the teachers if numbers were smaller, yet the methods do succeed, and some teachers I spoke with argued that they make it easier to teach large classes.

3. Tracking is not necessary in primary schools where the emphasis is on individual learning: British teachers are coming to see workable alternatives to ability grouping.

4. Informal methods work well not only with young children in the first years of school, but with older children, too. There are problems: the junior schools are slower to change, partly because they stand closer to the rigid secondary schools, and partly because it takes time and much experimenting to develop the kind of rich background of materials and methods the infant schools now possess. British curriculum projects are creating good open-ended materials, especially in science and math, for individual learning. Whatever the difficulties, it is clear that the junior schools are at their best when they continue along the freer lines of good infant schools.

5. Since nothing in schools happens in isolation, patterns of individual learning can develop in one area of the curriculum and spread to others. Thus for some British schools, art was the first subject in which children were encouraged to work on their own; others experimented with individual movement and mime and interpretive dancing in their physical education classes; some introduced the musical instruments devised for children by the German composer, Carl Orff; many schools are now discovering that mathematics is a great catalyst for change.

6. Everything depends on the teacher's confidence that children can learn with these methods. Where teachers and children are used to a strict timetable and traditional class-

PART TWO

THE STATE OF THE PROFESSION

Commentary

Since the report on infant schools first appeared in *The New Republic* in 1967, American interest in the British reforms has grown; a surprising number of American teachers and parents are familiarizing themselves with documents like the Plowden Report, *Children and Their Primary Schools*. A few of the most prominent local education authorities in England are now regularly swamped with American visitors; the swarms of educational tourists are becoming a nuisance. More usefully, various kinds of exchanges are springing up, and British teachers and advisors now regularly run workshops for colleagues on this side of the Atlantic.

In places as far apart in space and outlook as Rosebud,

Texas; Harlem; Vermont, Washington, D.C.; North Dakota; Boston; and Philadelphia, teachers of varying degrees of competence are attempting to work along the informal lines of the British primary schools. A number of private schools have been prompted to rethink their patterns of instruction, in some cases returning to practices current in the same schools in the 1930s and 1940s. Headstart centers often show traces of British influence, and one of several "models" that school systems may choose in the federal Follow Through program for Headstart graduates is adapted from the infant schools. The entire state of North Dakota has attempted to train and retrain its elementary school teachers in informal methods, apparently with some success. At City College in New York, Lillian Weber has established a string of infant-style classes in public schools. And Rosemary Williams, head of the superb Westfield school in Leicestershire (described in Chapter 1) came to the United States to organize an advisory team at the Educational Development Center in Newton, Massachusetts. (This team is, among other things, working with Follow Through schools.)

Often the vogue for British schools gives sanction to the work of Americans who have been teaching informally all along. Before anybody heard of infant schools, my wife did her student teaching under Nancy Verre, who was running an excellent informal first grade at the parent-sponsored New School in the Roxbury ghetto; now Miss Verre has joined Rosemary Williams's EDC team. Lore and Donald Rasmussen are another case in point. They emerged from curriculum reform efforts of the 1960s convinced that real change ought to mean a wholly different kind of classroom and a new role for the teacher. Operating entirely on their own, they have organized several training centers for teachers in the Philadelphia slums, out of which is coming excellent work.

To judge from the response, word of English practices has come at an opportune time. From very different perspectives, critics are questioning our schools' assumptions about learning, particularly young children's learning. Within the schools, there is a pedagogical vacuum. No one has suggested practical alternatives to existing methods; indeed, few reformers have deigned to speak directly to working teachers. The English example of a grass-roots reform carried out largely by people in the schools is attractive to our teachers, who are too often the victims of the general staff mentality of our innovators—witness the contemptuous efforts to devise "teacher-proof" curriculum materials. Outside the schools, disgruntled constituencies for change are growing. Blacks and other urban minorities are often receptive to new educational ideas, because they reject most aspects of the schools as they stand. And new classes of relatively well-off middle class parents want humane and open schools, even if they are a little vague about what such terms might mean pedagogically.

All these groups, but particularly teachers and parents, are starved for practical examples of good classrooms in operation. It is therefore natural that they concentrate on certain obvious external features of British classrooms: the rich stores of materials, often homemade, for children to play with and handle; the variety of activities going on at the same time; the absorption of children in their tasks; the curriculum arising from joint concerns and doings of teachers and children; the quality of math work, written expression, and art in the good schools; the freedom permitted both children and teachers; the altered, no less decisive role of the teacher as stage manager, catalyst, pace-setter, and guide for class and individual activities; the constant use of hallways and playgrounds, space that is wasted in our school buildings; and the experiments in a small number of

British authorities with "family grouping," mixing children of different ages in the same class.

This focus on specifics has been all to the good. In the great desert of educational discourse, accounts of real, live classrooms are like oases. But there is a tendency for Americans to linger uncritically on the surface features of British schools without paying much attention to the underlying prerequisites for change. Without some deeper perspective, the considerable interest in British schools could turn out to be another of those fads that regularly sweep across our educational landscape like prairie fires, leaving only charred grass behind.

Earlier, I mentioned certain prerequisites of the English reform: the belief that young children have distinct needs, distinct aptitudes for active learning in the concrete mode; the influence of various developmental theories; the relative autonomy of principals and teachers; the existence of advisors to support teachers and spread good work; the value of good work in setting new standards and in protecting a reform movement from being judged by its excesses. As more and more American schools grope toward informal teaching, we Americans should continually remind ourselves that the reform agenda has to include the entire school environment. We will have to talk about such seemingly small matters as the uncivilized way school lunches are served as well as such obviously important matters as patterns of administration. School bureaucracies, with their emphasis on administration at the expense of children, teachers, and parents, will have to be replaced by services that really support individual teachers in classrooms and principals in individual schools. Principals will have to see themselves, not as administrators, but as head teachers, whose main task is working with other teachers on the staff to improve the total human climate of the school.

As for the curriculum, there will have to be a unified

approach to children's learning, not the piecemeal, visionless, rag-and-bone curriculum we now have. The new curriculum will not emerge full-blown from planning agencies outside the schools; it will grow from careful work by teachers and children in classrooms over a long period of time. It cannot yet be entirely delineated, but its tentative outlines can be seen already in the practices of certain good teachers. In work with math apparatus and science materials, in children's art, movement, music, and writing, common threads will emerge more and more distinctly: active learning, engagement with materials, the centrality of expressiveness and communication; a new role for the teacher in organizing good learning experiences and environment. Quite properly, the importance of materials, the use of physical space, and informal scheduling should be stressed, but such innovations will fail to the extent we Americans forget that the decisive aspect of the school environment is people. Good teaching ought be proceed from the nature of children and their experiences toward more disciplined inquiry—starting with their lives here and now—on the assumption that childhood is something to be cherished, not romanticized or catered to, but valued for itself. All efforts will be vain unless they reflect a concern for the inescapable human context of learning, a conviction that the normal relations between adults and children are of supreme educational importance. All this has been said, perhaps too often. Philosophers and thinkers have repeatedly outlined the theoretical basis for a sound education with little effect. It remains for us to work out the theory in actual American classrooms. Neither theory nor glowing reports of good teaching will save us the effort of doing it ourselves.

By now I've visited a fair number of classrooms in America whose work has been inspired in one way or another by the British example. Some are as good as any you'll find in England; some are terrible parodies of sound education. Interestingly, the better ones have not been in affluent private or shoestring free schools, but in public schools—rare public schools where enterprising teachers get encouraged, instead of harassed, by the authorities. As a rough rule, American classrooms are more messy than English ones; I think this is a matter of experience—it takes time to realize the importance of housekeeping details. In general, American teachers working informally put more emphasis on formal instruction in reading than British teachers. This, they say, is a response to anxieties of parents, school authorities, and themselves. American teachers have one big advantage over the British in the later years of primary school: the sheer amount of gadgetry and science equipment available either commercially or through creative scrounging. This country has much more stuff for science-minded older children than the rather skimpily outfitted English junior schools.

Talking to American teachers actually working in informal settings is much like talking to their British colleagues. This is not true of Americans who have no clear picture in their minds of how such a classroom actually operates. Accounts of informal classrooms tend to fall into the stereotyped categories of a particular cultural cold war now raging in this society. This is, to oversimplify, a war between the straight lower and middle classes and the emancipated middle and upper middle classes. Partly it can be interpreted as a difference in whether one views life as essentially abundant, or essentially scarce. Older virtues of the regime of scarcity—discipline, order, thrift—are being challenged by the virtues of a new regime of abundance—openness, tolerance, the cultivation of feelings. Hip people like what they hear about English schools because they give children freedom, whereas straight people deplore what they imagine to be an absence of discipline and structure in informal classes.

Whichever side of this cultural divide you range yourself on, it is worth remembering that the issue of freedom, as opposed to structure, is not a central preoccupation of most British and American teachers I've met who successfully work with children in informal settings. Their concerns run on less ideological tracks. If you ask them about particular problems, they say they worry about how to reach a child who doesn't seem to be getting anything out of school; how to scavenge for materials, of which there are never enough; how to keep the momentum of an activity going when children's interests begin to flag; how to find time to work with one child who needs concentrated attention; how to set challenges that certain insecure children can meet in order to gain confidence.

If you watch good teachers in informal settings, it is perfectly clear that they make demands on the children, as well as on themselves. They feel responsible if the environment isn't stimulating enough; and they have some things to teach that they believe are of value. The teachers whose books I discuss in this volume share these traits in different ways: Herbert Kohl is a man of charm and immense enthusiasms, who sweeps a number of children along with him on an idea or project and is content to let the others wait until something else catches their fancy. Elwyn Richardson, in distant New Zealand, wants to help children develop a sense of values, confidence in their judgments of pottery, writing, and life. Frances Hawkins tries to discern a child's needs by reading the logic of his actions in the classroom, by paying him passionate attention.

In talk, in what they do, and in their rare writings, good teachers do not find that the question of freedom is at the core of their efforts with young children. They accept the real and legitimate authority of a teacher as an adult responsible for making a nurturing environment in which children and their talents can grow. Freeing children is part of the point; encouraging them to make significant choices is desirable, because often the choices reflect their needs, and, in any case, that is how they learn to develop initiative and think for themselves. By itself, however, freedom is an empty and cold educational aim. When we have many more good schools, and when our educational philosophy is more firmly grounded in actual practice, we will understand what a limited goal it was.

CHAPTER 3

VARIETIES OF GOOD PRACTICE...

A Philosophy Struggling to Be Heard

Frances Pockman Hawkins is a gifted teacher who spent every Thursday one spring semester with six deaf nursery school children in a Colorado public school. Although she was working within a classroom committed to a special program, bristling with designs and elaborate theoretical purposes, the authorities were wise enough to give Mrs. Hawkins a pretty free rein during her short visits. (They must have wondered about all the things she kept trucking into the school: equipment for making bubbles, tire pumps, plastic tubes, a hamster, food coloring, water trays, balances, and hundreds of other items to stock an informal classroom.)

Fortunately, she kept a daily notebook, a series of notes, photographs, and reflections on each class session—how it went, what children spent their time doing, what Mrs. Hawkins did, as well as what she refrained from doing, and what was in her mind as she taught.* Each entry starts off with a list of new equipment introduced—there's an appendix on all the stuff, with useful notes—and then a narrative of the day's teaching follows.

Almost every attempt to describe what goes on in a good classroom fails, and every reader will come to items in her log where he feels he is not being told enough, or is being told too much. Nonetheless, Mrs. Hawkins is a shrewd observer, and her individual sketches of the children are delightful. She is keen to distill an occasional abstract principle from her experiences, and passages in these notes have the muffled, murky, and complex quality that nearly always marks the efforts of good teachers to pin down their art in words and general terms. The brilliance poises on the edge of portentousness, and only her massive common sense and her instinct for detail keeps her upright. The reader is standing on a heaving deck that is likely to pitch him from soap bubbles and giggles to very different levels of discourse: "Attention is a close cousin of love and one does not speak of training someone to love, but rather of providing the right setting."

What emerges is an original and fascinating sketch of what one experienced teacher is thinking about as she teaches. Mrs. Hawkins has illuminating things to say about her deaf charges, but this is really about teaching all children, rich or poor, wounded or whole. This work has one particular virtue that few books about informal teaching possess: it really concentrates on what an adult has to con-

*Frances Pockman Hawkins, *The Logic of Action: From a Teacher's Notebook*, Mountain View Center for Environmental Education, University of Colorado, 1969.

tribute to children's learning. While Mrs. Hawkins believes as passionately as anyone in environments where children are free to pursue their own learning independently, Mrs. Hawkins does not believe that such environments come about by accident. A teacher has the responsibility for choosing the materials, managing the stage. As the children learn, as they choose, the teacher still has further decisions to make: when to step in, when to keep quiet, what kind of help to give. It is an elusive process.

At first, for example, she sees that her children, perhaps because they are deaf, cling to routine more than most four-year-olds she has met; they remind her of older children, trained by the schools to rely less and less on their own experiences. So she deliberately interrupts the expected routine, to wean them from the ordinary and get them used to novelties:

> Whatever I did was immediately copied, and, as one must when this happens, I had to change what I started as quickly as possible, providing more than one way to copy, thus sanctioning and inviting variety. . . . When a group of fives produces replica upon replica of one paper ornament, it is time to watch for and dignify, perhaps hanging from a mobile, one child's "mistake"—one hard to copy and thus conducive to the production of still more mistakes.

The purpose of the enterprise is to help a child "regain and develop this capacity to probe and test, to summon his sleeping resources of imagery, control, and understanding—in short, to learn, and not to memorize." One avenue to a classroom where this is likely to happen is the teacher's own interests. If the teacher herself is exploring the material and not just watching it being used, the odds of engaging a child's mind increase. There are, as Mrs. Hawkins demonstrates, innumerable things that adults and four-year-olds can explore together. She enjoyed watching water bubbles in the plastic tubes "falling upward," and argues convincingly that this shared interest is more valuable to the children than any amount of mere adult praise for their inventions. Her account suggests some of the richness inherent in good, open-ended science materials.

She is always conscious of herself as stage manager and catalyst. Sometimes the role is straightforward and simple, as when Patty takes up the attribute blocks to get away from the crowd and work on her own: "I protected her right to work there alone." Other times, as in planning to introduce new materials, there are many things to consider. Two long soundings from Mrs. Hawkins's flow of thought will have to suffice. Here she is thinking about artificial food coloring:

> The materials here are still inherently new to most children and esthetically vivid. It has been my experience that there is more enjoyment and exploration if the introduction of food color is "structured." On this particular morning . . . I made another judgment. A time for quieter activity with the teacher involved was needed. Had the early part of morning followed another kind of pattern, I might have cancelled these plans. On a Monday morning, for example, after a cold and confining weekend, I have found children so deeply in need of self-direction in familiar paths, with adults far in the background, that I have to put away "structured" plans. Guidance at such times courts trouble. . . .

And here she is thinking about setting up balances:

> I wanted to introduce them, not head-on, but tangentially and in sequence with enough sure-fire old stuff so that the children would not rush all at once to the balances just because they were new. Such structuring has at least two justifications: it allows a child sufficient time to use a new piece of equipment without having at once to share or wait turns. Materials such as this yardstick-cum-weights-on-upright are more likely to "speak" to a child when there is time for continued experimen-

tation. In addition . . . [this] approach provides a teacher the luxury of observation. . . .

In time, most of the children follow their separate paths to the realization that not all things have to be demonstrated. Some, perhaps, knew this all along but were not used to acting on it in practice. Mrs. Hawkins's role is built up from thousands of small concerns: making sure to take pains in presenting the delicate acetate gels-colored sheets to look through, so the children learn to treat them with proper care; remembering to start cleaning up early enough so the children have time to unwind. Some who read her notes may say that all this simply reflects the fact that Mrs. Hawkins is a remarkable person. That goes without saying. Yet many of the concerns she touches are to some degree those of all good teachers of all children of all ages. The ability comes naturally to some, and by experience to others; each teacher would describe how he works in a different way. These notes don't pretend to tell teachers what to teach, although they are full of suggestions. In their tentative, unfinished way, they present a series of working illustrations of principles in practice. Through them a philosophy of education is struggling to be heard, although in the absence of many more such classrooms and first-hand teachers' accounts, we will never be able to articulate it realistically, without dogma or cant.

Harlem Sixth Grade

Herbert Kohl's simple narrative of his experiences with a sixth-grade class in Harlem describes what happens as one teacher and his children respond to each other, and he gathers his nerve to alter his way of teaching.* It is the top

*The material quoted herein is reprinted by permission of The World Publishing Company from *36 Children* by Herbert Kohl. An NAL book. Copyright ©1967 by Herbert Kohl.

sixth-grade class, but only five or six out of the thirty-six children can read a sixth-grade book and more than half are reading at fourth-grade level when he begins. Inexperienced, he first sticks to assigned texts and tries to maintain a strict schedule with separate periods for different subjects. He wages a private war with himself over discipline, fearing he will lose control. In retrospect, he sees that this tightness with time and material had nothing to do with how much had to be learned in the school year or the amount of ground the class had to cover, for the truth was that after five full years the children had learned very little anyway.

Gradually building up his confidence he makes his own accommodation to discipline and so do the children. He starts letting them take ten-minute breaks between subjects, when they can play the piano, chess, and checkers or read. At the end of the second day's break, the class resists going back to work, but he insists. He believes that failure on this point would have been disastrous, because the children had made a bargain and had to keep it. (Perhaps its was important for him to know that the students could keep bargains.)

Things worked out, painfully:

> I remember days getting home from school angry at myself, confused by my behavior in the classroom, my ranting and carping, my inability to let the children alone. I kept saying "That's not me, that's not me." For a while, as I learned to teach, the me in the classroom was an alien and hostile being.

But he overcomes the fear that if one child got out of control the whole class would follow:

> I let an insult pass and discovered that the rest of the class didn't take up the insult; I learned to say nothing when Ralph returned from pacing the halls or when Alvin refused to do

arithmetic. The children did not want to be defiant, insulting, idle; nor were they any less afraid of chaos than I was.

He is never able to line everybody up at three o'clock. Sadly, he reports that one boy he couldn't reach left the class. But teacher and children learn to live with each other, which is as close as anybody comes to solving the discipline problem.

There are many profound reflections on teaching scattered through *36 Children*, but one small and almost peripheral illustration of Kohl's awareness of the complexities will have to suffice. This concerns a teacher's need for privacy, a separate existence outside the classroom, even for a year or two away from teaching. At one point he has the children over to his apartment after school. (To some teachers and administrators this in itself would be scandalous, like fraternizing with the enemy in no-man's-land.) The visits are a success, but he finds, finally, that he has to restrict them to one day a week. The children are angry when he tells them he needs his own life. (I've met good teachers who could not appreciate this, or if they could, were unable to do anything about it. They never set apart any aspect of themselves, they gave their classes everything, and you sensed that they were being scooped hollow. In the end, they were left trying to live vicariously through the children, which is not enough.)

36 Children is an important document, because it shows how a teacher abandons the usual classroom methods, creating an informal class where children work on their own, where they are offered choices about what to do, where they generate a good deal of the curriculum themselves including some extraordinary writing. He shows us their poems, myths, sly fables, comic strips, autobiographies, essays, and wildly inventive science fiction novels.

36 Children is an eloquent anthology testifying to the creative energy of these Harlem students.

A class in which the teacher simply likes the children and a class where the children are stimulated to do first-rate work are not at all the same things. *36 Children* sheds light on the difference. Its lessons apply to suburbs as well as slums, for very few schools anywhere in America regularly permit children to choose the content of their writing, and children's literature is rarely read with the respect and attention it must have in order to thrive. Kohl claims no originality for his discovery that children can write. Other teachers have discovered the same thing. People learn to use words, to want to use words well by trying to get across something they want to say to an audience they wish to reach and move. Children learn to write by writing. (But, as he says, they will not write if they are afraid to talk.) His example is relevant to every level of education, from first grade through graduate school, but it hits with particular force because his class is composed of black and Puerto Rican children, who, we are often told, lack vocabulary, are unable to handle abstractions, learn mainly from physical, rather than mental, activity, and so on. In fact, his children like to write and have plenty to say. Not all are gifted writers, though some are; many of them, like many adults, have only a single important story to tell, to write and to rewrite. Yet, "all of them . . . seemed to become more alive through their writing."

In changing from a formal to a freer class, Kohl is driven by desperation, not by any vision of proper teaching. For six or seven weeks he struggles with the assigned books; it is hopeless. He is bored, and so are the children. Occasionally, the class comes to life: a discussion of the Patterson-Liston fight, a conversation about the word "psyche" that leads the astonished children to consider the idea that language and words have altered over time, have a history. "You mean words change?" "You mean one day the way we talk—you know, with words like cool and dig and soul—may be all right?" They are fascinated by the myth of Cupid and Psyche. So Kohl drops the dreary social studies text (*How We Became Modern America*) and teaches them about words, myths, and periods of history that interest him. Social studies becomes a free period, a long break in which the teacher overwhelms the class with books and projects, and lets them find out what they like. There are no reports to file or set numbers of pages to read. There are books on architecture, the Greeks, mythology, Mesopotamia, early man; books on World War II for a set of war buffs, art books for a boy who draws constantly, *The Bobbsey Twins* and novels like Dorothy Sterling's *Mary Jane*, the story of a Negro girl who integrates a white school.

As they begin choosing, the teachers finds that he can take time to observe and get some idea of what intrigues them. A few boys get interested in science and tell him of an unused cache of science equipment somewhere in the school. Others know where they can lay hands on a record player. Kohl brings his records to class, and the class introduces him to Moms Mabley. Soon they are telling him about the neighborhood, then they begin to write about it. The papers aren't marked; no one has to write. This is, he says, probably the first time they had ever written to say something that mattered to them:

> I live 62 E. 120st My neighborhood is not so bad. Everyone has children in the block. Many of the children are Spanish. Some of them run around nude and dirty. Some of the houses are so dirty you would be scare to come in the door. Sometimes the drunks come out and fight. . . . Many of the people in the block drink so much they don't have time for the children. The chil-

dren have no place to play they have the park but the parents
don't care enough to take them. Now you have a idea of what
my block is like.

Kohl finds himself running a very different kind of class.
The free social-studies period expands to a free day. Each
morning he puts an assignment on the board, and the class
has a choice of reading and writing, or doing the assignment. Writing is private, unless the author wants to make it
public; the children are encouraged to work at one task
until the momentum is lost. Some are upset by the absence
of routine and miss the comfort of doing things by rote.
Their teacher often wavers, too, and thinks about going
back to formal teaching.

The first book he is allowed to see is an autobiography
by Maurice, eleven years old:

> This story is about a boy named Maurice and his life as it is
> and how it will be. Maurice is in the six grade now, but this
> story, will tell you about his past, present and future. . . . When
> I was born I couldn't see at first, but like all families my father
> was waiting outside after a hour or so I could see shadows. . . .

Robert Jackson, the artist, begins an astonishing literary
output with a book clearly influenced by his reading about
Greece. *A Barbarian Becomes a Greek Warrior* is a violent
adventure story about a weakling with "the strength of
luck" who grows into a great hero: "One day in Ancient
Germany, a boy was growing up. His name was Pathos. He
was named after this Latin word because he had sensitive
feelings. In Ancient Germany the Romans had their vast
empire. . . ."

Different children respond to different kinds of writing
and try out new voices and modes. After hearing fables
from Aesop and Thurber, one wrote:

> Once upon a time there was a pig and a cat. The cat kept
> saying you old dirty pig who want to eat you. And the pig

replied when I die I'll be made use of, but when you die you'll just rot. The cat always thought he was better than the pig. When the pig died he was used as food for the people to eat. When the cat died he was buried in old dirt.

Moral: Live dirty die clean.

Some fashion myths, mingling Cyclops and Zeus with Superman and Wonder Woman. The most impressive—"awesome" is, quite properly, the word his teacher uses—is a long, unfinished fragment of the Elektra myth by Alvin Curry, Jr., which opens: "This story called Elektra is of the deepest passion and the deepest hope of avengeance of her father's death. . . ."

The children produce a magazine, *AND*, which has many fine things, including illustrated mythologies by Robert Jackson, and Marie Forde's poem, "The Junkies":

> When they are
> in the street
> they pass it
> along to each
> other but when
> they see the
> police they would
> just stand still
> and be beat
> so pity ful
> that they want
> to cry.

The school's authorities, who in most respects seem to have left Mr. Kohl to his own devices, thought that *AND* contained too much terror and violence and recommended that the class study a fifth-grader's sticky poem on shopping with Mom. The assistant principal's reaction to *AND* was to offer its creators a lesson in proofreading.

Kohl's portrait of the New York City schools is devastating, but done with justice and a certain amount of pity as well as rage. For instance: "It was difficult not to feel the general chaos—to observe the classes without teachers, the children wandering aimlessly, sometimes wantonly through the halls, disrupting classes, intimidating, extorting, yet being courted by the administration: 'Please don't make trouble, anything you want, but no trouble.'

In the spring, Kohl demonstrates what he thinks of the system by doing something that radically contradicts its premises, something that many teachers in slum schools would regard as unprofessional. (If teachers really were professionals, they would be loyal primarily to their immediate students and not to their superiors or the school system.) He explains to his children that they are going to have to take reading and (at that time in New York) IQ tests which determine placement in junior high school and thus their whole future. He takes out their records and tells them their past scores. They are angry and shocked, for no one in all their years in school had ever told them frankly how low they stood. In this, the top sixth-grade class in the school, only two children have IQ scores above 100; the majority are in the eighty to ninety range. The class asks what can be done, and Kohl does what teachers of middle-class children often, and teachers of slum children almost never, do: he teaches them how to take tests. (As he explains, many teachers in slum schools feel that their failures with children are excised if objective tests establish that the children are failures.) He gets old tests and drills the class for several weeks in the tricky art of following instructions. The children object to the boring drill, but he makes them be realistic. Their superb sixth-grade work doesn't matter; they'll go nowhere in junior high school unless the test scores are satisfactory. He teaches them the different kinds of test questions and gets them to see that they mustn't be too clever and outsmart tests. Children sometimes have trouble learning that a test has only one right answer, and that the task is to figure out what the person who made the test expects, and not simply what seems like a reasonable answer. They have to be trained to think on the test's level, not on their level. They were; "they agreed to be dull for the sake of their future."

There was too little time to prepare for the IQ tests, and only ten in the class scored over 100, one girl getting 135. But reading tests later on in the year showed the results of determined coaching. Most of the class jumped one to three years, a few were at a fifth-grade level, twelve were on the seventh-grade level, and eight read on levels between eighth and twelfth grades.

The reading tests were a victory of sorts. The year was certainly a victory for Kohl and his children. He hadn't created the visionary social studies course he once imagined teaching, which would instruct children "to be able to persist, revolt, and change things in our society and yet not lose their souls in the process." But he had done wonderful things. The children had learned to read widely and to like reading, and they had discovered that they could write, to touch on the more obvious consequences of their encounter with a gifted and warm teacher. But this is a tragic book as well as the story of success. For Kohl follows the careers of the children after they left the sixth grade in 1963. The returns are far from complete, but there is enough evidence to justify one child's mournful observation, "Mr. Kohl, one good year isn't enough." Despite the children's tenacious desire to finish school and the foolish hopes and dreams that kept them going long after the pointlessness of school was evident, they came back bewildered to their sixth-grade teacher to report discouragement and steady demoralization. One girl made it to a prep school in New England,

paying a heavy psychic price for making it in the white
world. A handful of other girls endured. The attrition rate
among the boys was sickening. Robert Jackson, whose
drawings and writings adorn *36 Children*, quit the High
School of Music and Art. (When Kohl went to inquire why,
he met a guidance counselor whose office was full of black
students. "You know we're very good to ——— here," she
whispered, writing the word "Negroes" on a pad.) Michael,
who once worked on a novel, *Frankenstein Meets Cyclops
and Psyche*, still dreamed of becoming a writer. He wanted
to master the craft, but school was irrelevant, and he was
selling newspapers for a living. Another boy, Ralph, was
"beginning to look like those permanent dwellers in junkies' paradise." In letters and writings to his teacher, Alvin
Curry records the downward path to wisdom. Subsequent
teachers treated him as illiterate; yet gloomily he continued
to write. This is from his "The Condemned Building:"

> There is a leaky faucet, going with a steady drip of water, there
> is no recreation whatsoever where a person can spend his leisure
> time, but there is something to look at, the walls which have
> plaster peeling, which suggests different moods that a person
> may be in, the walls are so arranged that they suggest different
> scenes like maybe a scene of you gradually graduating from
> boyhood to man when the mirage has passed you notice that
> the windows are uneasily pitch black suggesting for you maybe
> a private hell where you can satisfy your own desires . . . you
> step into the outside where you ask yourself why is this build-
> ing condemned, where a person can find his inner self. Why do
> they condemn this building where man can find out what he is
> or will be.
>   Why do they condemn Life?

As the toll mounts, Kohl is forced to ask himself whether he
did his children a favor by teaching them to write and think,
whether it was good to create expectations that schools did

not live up to. He hopes he can find a way to continue teaching children, but he will be less certain that he can save them next time. What he will be able to do, at least, is ease "the burden of being alive in the United States to-day."

36 Children presents an aspect of the social tragedy now engulfing this country, but it is much more than simply another book with the same message we have heard and ignored often before.

Each child has signed his teacher's memory with a characteristic bit of wit, a way of talking or writing, a special bravado. The book is tragic, but it is its triumph to demonstrate the stubborn individuality of these children, who, with their intelligence and their promise are so much bigger than the small, mean fates stalking them. In Harlem, iron traps are set and waiting for the young flesh, but there is a gaiety in their lives, and there are gestures of deep courtesy, too, and these are also part of the rich, increasingly bitter truth *36 Children* tells us.

Utopian Bulletin from New Zealand

Elwyn S. Richardson's *In the Early World* is a utopian bulletin on twelve years of work in one tiny country school in northern New Zealand.* It may be the best book about teaching ever written. Certainly it's one of the most beautifully designed. Reproductions of children's art of an astonishing quality fill its pages—wood and linoleum cuts, pottery, and fabrics, as well as writing. It is a densely constructed work, not easy to read. In different puzzling contexts, Richardson thinks and rethinks his ideas. The reader seems

*Elwyn S. Richardson, *In The Early World,* Pantheon Books, a Division of Random House, Inc. Copyright © 1964 by the New Zealand Council for Educational Research.

to be sitting with him, listening in on the effort of recollec-
tion as he turns an accumulation of children's work over in
his hands, trying to figure out what went into its making.

It takes time for the reader to understand that a long
account of how the class took up pottery is meant to be
emblematic of a whole style of teaching. Clay of various
grades lay in deposits near the school, and Richardson and
the children tested samples to see which kinds were good
to work with. They built a small brick kiln and pottery
became a standard activity in the school. Messing around,
the children slowly learned the limits of the material—you
couldn't build wet clay too high or it would collapse. At
first, they tended toward fussy overdecoration of pots, producing a mass of derivative and clichéd work. When they
showed him their poor early efforts, Richardson found
small aspects to praise, solitary virtues to single out. The
important thing that was emerging, Richardson saw only in
retrospect, was a sense of values, the idea that some work
was better than other work, and that children could learn
to make such judgments. He tried to get them to examine
why a pot was better, but they were content to decide that
it just was, and deserved to be put in a special display area
that in time enveloped the whole classroom. Discussions
contributed to setting a standard. (Later, Richardson worried about this procedure, but "that was after I saw that
there were different standards of values developing among
the children.") They began to take each other's work seriously, in a critical spirit. This pot was too heavy and not as
good as your last one, one boy told another; the lips
weren't drawn in enough, but certain strokes were lovely.
Quality improved: "As soon as judgment begins, as in the
selection of some better [examples] from the mass of work,
the influences of the inferior are no longer felt so much
and there is a need . . . to re-order . . . thinking." Looking

back, Richardson felt that a great deal of his early teaching was ineffective, because he did not know how to discriminate between good work and bad (he knew nothing about pottery to start with), and because he failed to see the process of learning to discriminate as one of the points of the whole enterprise.

With the smaller and less confident children (the school took students from five to fifteen years of age) he found he had to arrange matters more carefully. Plaster molds into which clay could be pressed were useful because they enabled children to make adequate pottery right away without first having to master the tricky art of laying down coils of clay to form the foundation of a pot. On their own, the children experimented with textures, pressing wood, bark, and seashells into the clay to form designs. They discovered a few bold strokes could be more effective than elaborate decoration; they became confident enough to use line, mass, and color in abstract ways, A dozen or so children became real potters. Their work is handsomely displayed in the book's illustrations.

Pottery was where Richardson began. After a time it influenced other work, especially in crafts—not writing, however, which the children continued to regard as a chore. Once in a while there would be an apt caption for a picture, but Richardson was appalled by what the children produced when they tried "poetry." Their whole notion of written expression was stunted; what writing they had been exposed to was unrelated to any of their experiences and totally alien to how they talked. Fine writing was poetry, which was about set, usually esoteric or fey subjects. It had to rhyme: "The thrush sings all day/but it doesn't have any pay."

With pottery and crafts, discussions had improved the children's work; this was not true of writing, partly because there was so little promising material to begin with. A small section of a poor linocut could be singled out for praise, but Richardson found little to note in the children's first labored literary efforts. A few children, misinterpreting his anxiety over quality, attempted to please him by writing up storms of turgid poetry. He would pick out one good sentence from these lengthy, labored efforts, hoping to encourage shorter pieces.

He took to collecting vivid sentences, even single images from things the children said or wrote, copying them for display. (The smaller children were a fund of images—they looked at puddles and found "the upside down world.") He read the class translations of short poems, Japanese haiku. Working small, in bits of prose, each child could have the sense of doing something well. And, as with the pottery, there came to be a basis for discussing the quality of work. A whole genre of short poems evolved, which the children called "picture poems," unrhymed lyrical statements expressing one or two thoughts at most. Irene, 13, wrote:

> The pine tree stands
> With cracked sooted arms
> With stumped branches
> Rotted into the ground.

These formed a starting point for talking about longer efforts, which began to reappear in many forms. When the class read

> Under the blind seawater
> The bubble fingered seaweeds
> Dance and run around in airy water
>
> They never seem to sleep
> And never seem to break the surface
> Or dance too heavily.

The sun does never beat upon them
And they are never afraid of a drop of water
Because it is well and truly wet down there.

And on the darkly shaded rocks
The limpets spit and cling.

they selected the first two verses as poems in themselves, rejected the third as weak (among other faults, it talked of matters about which the poet was ignorant), and suggested that the last verse stand on its own as a brief statement.

It was not enough to consider the value of a finished piece of prose or pottery; it was more helpful if the children talked as they worked. "Why no leaves?" somebody would ask. "I don't like your two figures. They're better than the ones in your last painting, David." "I like your story, but I was disappointed you didn't say more about things you people were talking about after lights went out. . . ." "I like that (a poem on moths) very much. . . . Stuart knows a lot about moths. He writes as if he is a moth. . . ." Richardson found himself impressed by their ability to judge work dispassionately. Now and then something one of them considered important was rejected, but usually "they were kind to children who rarely shone in their expression and saw that what was 'good' for one person was not the same 'good' for another. . . ."

Sometimes he set exercises, which produced effective, if contrived writing: describe water going down a drain, put your chin on a level with the grass and tell how things look, characterize a visitor to the school, or write down, as fast as possible, all the thoughts that run through your head in ten minutes. (This last produced raw material, ideas and images the children could later work on.)

As they wrote nature studies, stories, narratives, poems, autobiographical fragments, fantasies, the children perfected a system. One would decide which of his works were to be read out loud and discussed. The class then selected the best, which were bound into a series of school magazines, each bearing a new title.

Richardson says he seldom tried to get the whole class interested in the same thing; the idea was to interest a child in something and then encourage him to pursue it. In time, children's topics encroached on his formal class lessons, but he still gave lessons for the whole class when he felt there was something they all needed to know. Some days he left school feeling he had taught too much: other days he thought he should have given more direction then he did. (He kept notes on errors that individual children repeated.)

Children's topics overrode subjects, as well as the timetable. Richardson found that stories and picture-poems would suggest ideas for paintings and cuts. Sometimes he suggested that a child paint what he hadn't said much about in a story. Particularly with some of the Maori children, good art work led to much better work in other subjects. A few flourished by an almost obsessive concentration on a single theme: one painted darkness and wrote about night; another worked and reworked, in prose, cuts, peoms, and paintings, the discovery of a dead bird.

In the Early World is an extraordinary anthology of children's writing, but Richardson is careful to underscore the time it took for many children to write anything of value; only a few, he says, ever developed a distinctive style. What was missing for many was simply stimulation: something to write about. The best work arose from chance encounters: some starlings nesting near the school led to an abundant harvest of writing and painting; a boy's clay portrait led to an impressive series of heads and masks. True quality was rare even in his school, Richardson felt, because so little school work ever captured experience on the wing.

His country school never offered what could be called a balanced curriculum: his own absorptions, nature studies, crafts, and writing, clearly predominated. But *In the Early World* is the most thoughtful portrait I've come across of a school in which children are writing, talking, and thinking, and not simply going through a set of motions called education.

The temptation never to believe what anybody says about schools is strong, yet this account from New Zealand is convincing. Its few ideas are densely wound around examples of actual work on the part of children who seem very alive. You are inclined to accept the spirit of Richardson's testimony when, at the end, he struggles to put matters into words and finishes with some old and much abused formulas:

> I saw that I had to teach as much as I could when opportunities arose, and that this was a better kind of teaching than I had known when I was following through topic after topic. If I did not teach at such times, the work became poor and lifeless. . . . The series of developments taught me, too, that I must use environment to the full and encourage individual expression rather than class. This meant more individual and small group observation. . . .

Teachers and Writers Collaborative

A small organization called the Teachers and Writers Collaborative has been placing professional writers in classrooms to work with children and teachers, on a regular basis, not as performers or visiting firemen. Operating mainly in New York, the project also runs teacher workshops, develops some materials, and puts out a newsletter in the form of a magazine. The newsletter prints class diaries, reflections and notes on teaching and composition, and, above all, masses of student writing—poems, blues lyrics, *haiku*, comic strips, fables, mock advertisements ("Scrubbly Bubbly guarantees your nose will fall off"), bestiaries, word collages and printograms (words run together to form a drawing, a peace dove, for example), interviews, even a parody of a Dick and Jane reader. The newsletter comes out fitfully, and the quality is uneven. But I'd like to see it or something like it get known as a forum where students, writers, and teachers could publish and find out what others are up to. None of the underground high-school publications is doing that so far; many have bite and topicality, but they are too short-lived and too narrow in their interests to be concerned with developing students' writing. The editors of high-school underground papers know that our schools don't encourage writing, and, from the perspective of their experience, they must find it hard to believe that adults and students can meet with common profit, as they do in the Collaborative.

Teachers who come across the newsletter will not have revealed to them a technique for getting good writing. It hardly needs to be said again that no fixed methods can be abstracted from a particular classroom experience and transferred intact to another setting. Yet teachers in various times and places have found certain ideas useful, particularly in getting started. Some of the Collaborative writers, for example, hit upon the fact that children are intrigued by "found" poems, poems formed by picking sentences at random from books and signs and putting them together. Students are surprised to learn that they already know poetry, street poetry like the skip rope chant: "Apples in the summer/Peaches in the fall/Don't let your mother catch you/Kissing in the hall." And there are old formulas that sometimes prove helpful in giving uncertain children a framework on which to build a first piece of writing, such

as a work constructed on the theme: "I used to be a_____,
but now I'm a_____."

One section in a Collaborative newsletter does something rare: it presents teachers talking about ideas that fell
flat. As a rule, educators shun autopsies, so it's refreshing
to have a teacher set the tone for a discussion of one
botched class with a rueful quote from T.S. Eliot's lugubri-
ous parody of Marlowe: "I used to be a taxidermist; but
that was in another country, and besides, the animals were
dead." We are told of a class in which two teachers got
students excited about an idea, and nothing happened:
". . . perhaps too much of their liveliness was channeled into the preliminaries . . . both assignments began with too
concrete an idea in the teacher's mind of what he wanted
. . . the students had no choice but to psych out what the
teacher might have in mind. . .."

One of the Collaborative poets, Kenneth Koch, did an
extended stint teaching at PS 61 on the Lower East Side of
New York. He has put together a fresh, lively anthology of
his kids' writing, in which he tells how he started with
poems written collectively by the whole class, after which
the children branched out on their own.* They did poems
in which every line states a wish—a repetitive device that
automatically gives poems a certain rough, sing-song structure. The little children took these very seriously; sixth
graders, on the other hand, wrote lines like: "I wish JV
would turn into a ruffles potato chip." Koch found that
certain suggestions were helpful in priming the pump: avoid
rhyme, make the poem crazy, or silly, put a comparison, or
a noise, or a color, in every line. Some of the late comparison poems nicely mix senses and meanings.

*From *Wishes, Lies, Dreams: A Way of Teaching Children Poetry* by Kenneth
Koch. Copyright ©1970 by Kenneth Koch. Reprinted by permission of Random
House, Inc.

Snow is as white as the sun shines.
The sky is as blue as a waterfall.
A rose is as red as a beating of drums.
The clouds are as white as the busting of a firecracker.
A tree is as green as a roaring lion.

The process of writing was cumulative. From poems about wishes, comparisons, colors, and noises, the class moved on to poems about dreams, and, sure enough, these incorporated wishes, comparisons, colors, and noises. Metaphor poems flourished after a child mistakenly wrote about a "swan of bees," instead of a "swarm," and students began playing with words: "I had a dream of my banana pillow/And of my pyjamas of oranges."

One thing Koch noticed—familiar to teachers working in all the arts—is how much children draw from each other's work. If one student wrote: "I used to be a fish/ But now I'm a nurse," another listened and played variations:

I used to be a nurse
But now I am a dead person
I always was Mr. Coke
But now I am Mrs. Seven Up.

Through what at first were fairly mechanical exercises, the class developed what amounted to a homemade literary tradition based on familiar sorts of poems they had tried, or at least seen others try. Up to this point, Koch found, the best poetry to read to stimulate further effort was other children's work. Thereafter, however, some were able to listen to adult poetry and make use of it. When Koch read Wallace Stevens' "Harmonium" poems, echoes of Stevens emerged in the children's poetry: "Owl go like who and who. Who and who and who . . ." Or: "The sun had a glare of glass in it." Some lovely work followed a reading of poems by D.H. Lawrence.

They had fun with poems and words in Spanish, which

many of the children spoke, with sestinas and pantoums, and with "I seem to be/But really I am" poems. They wrote poems in which every line had to be a lie. Out of this last assignment, for reasons I don't quite understand, came the following extraordinary poem entitled *The Dawn of Me* by Jeff Morley, a fifth-grader:

I was born nowhere
And I live in a tree
I never leave my tree
It is very crowded
I am stacked up right against a bird
But I won't leave my tree
Everything is dark
No light!
I hear the bird sing
I wish I could sing
My eyes, they open
And all around my house
The Sea
Slowly I get down in the water
The cool blue water
Oh and the space
I laugh swim and cry for joy
This is my home
For Ever

Somewhat to his surprise, Koch learned that his youngsters enjoyed writing poems in the classroom rather than at home, which was too close to being homework. The noise didn't bother them, and they seemed to like the idea of writing together. His job, as he saw it, was to help them with hard words, and give them ideas, applause, encouragement: "So I was useful in the classroom for getting the children in a good mood to write and then for keeping them going. And they were useful to each other in creating a humming and buzzing creative ambience. . ."

Marvin Hoffman, who runs the Collaborative, is modest

about what it has accomplished. By being small and special, it inches around the whole question of teaching credentials for its writers. It certainly hasn't cracked all the problems of dealing with the beleaguered New York school system. The biggest obstacles are in the high schools, where fear of student uprisings and repression are rampant, and censorship of student expression is the rule. It is a small, but significant indication of the desperate state of the high schools that a project like the Collaborative can't generally work in them, even though it has found plenty of elementary and junior high schools to work in. (Nor is this true only of New York's high schools.) The Collaborative also suffers from the enfeebling ailments of enterprises in education and the arts that depend on charity. What limited funds there are, often are disbursed on the questionable assumption that a good project will automatically find its own base of support after a limited period of sponsorship. A string of sponsors has given the Collaborative grants, including the National Endowment for the Humanities, but prospects for raising more money are doubtful.

There is a division in the project between, mainly, the black and Puerto Rican poets and writers and their white colleagues. Broadly, it might be called political, and it reflects a climate that no one in today's city schools can escape. The black and Puerto Rican writers are particularly interested in helping students become more conscious of themselves as black and Puerto Rican, part of a cultural and political movement. The whites tend to focus on writing.

A more prosaic problem confronting any such enterprise as the collaborative is recruiting writers who can teach, and who can work with teachers. It will come as no surprise to literary historians that some writers can't teach; or that some aren't good at dealing with other adults.

Teachers are always being victimized by experts of one sort or another who sweep into their classrooms, tell them how it should be done, and then depart, pocketing their consultant fees. The resentment is keener when the expert turns out to be a flop with the children. But even when the expert does have something to offer, as the Collaborative writers do, he needs tact and diplomacy, qualities always in short supply in our schools.

The contents of the Collaborative's newsletter naturally reflect the concerns of professional writers, and especially of poets. The children's writing is largely literary, in the sense of taking place in a separate realm, consciously poetic at its best—as in Jeff Morley's poem—and cute and artificial at its worst. It is probably not the Collaborative people's fault that there is no decent writing on science or math projects—they are working with the schools as they exist after all—but the newsletter generally lacks good examples of children's prose about real experiences, in or out of school.

The truth is, I think, that poetry is not everyone's cup of tea. Most of us would not write consistently well if we were called upon to make poems every day for a special period in an ordinary, bare classroom (even if encouraged by such an engaging man as Kenneth Koch). Some would do pretty well, and for a while most of us might learn something about poetic forms and poets—we would certainly profit from participating in the common literary endeavor that was Koch's main achievement at PS 61. The experience of trying on the poet's role would be good for us. But after a while I suspect we would lack things to write about; we would need more stimulation, experiences to feed on. This is particularly true of children, but it also holds for adults: think of people in those creative writing classes, all dressed up, with no place to go. Many of us

would tire of the specialty called poetry and the class period called writing.

This is another way of saying that the Collaborative's
admirable effort runs into difficulties that all specializations
meet in schools. I visited IS 201 in Harlem, the intermedi-
ate school which has been the battleground for so many of
the skirmishes in the struggle for community control. The
two art teachers in the school, Irene Mayson and Patricia
Lamendola, got their children absorbed in West African art,
with astounding results: papier-mâché masks of all sorts and
colors, dyed fabrices, paintings, lino cuts, detailed wood-
cuts, and wonderful carvings in mahogany, masks, friezes,
abstract designs. Some of the work, especially in wood, was
as beautiful as I've seen in any school and amazing to come
across in a junior high school, since they are not as a rule
very interesting places. As you looked over this gorgeous
stuff, you searched for a way of applying some of the
energy that went into it to all the other subjects taught in
the building. The excellent principal of IS 201, Ronald
Evans, would be the first to concede that nothing elsewhere
matches the quality of the art.

Obviously, having first-rate art teachers is a blessing
for IS 201, just as the Collaborative writers would be good
for any school. It is beneficial and unusual for children to
come across adults who really know an academic subject; it
is probably more beneficial for them to meet grown-ups
who are good at their respective craft and can teach what
they live for. (This applies to lawyers and carpenters, as
much as to artists, writers, and musicians.) But it is disap-
pointing to see the way school routines close around the
specialists they do get, isolating them from the rest of the
curriculum. (In bad schools, this isolation protects the specialists and often leaves their classrooms little islands of
life.) If the Collaborative survives, I hope it can cooperate

more with teachers in remaking the school curriculum entirely. It should in any case by paying more attention to teachers. In the meantime, Koch's account and the Collaborative's work are additional proofs of a truth that has to be trumpeted until the school walls come tumbling down: all children can write, lyricially, playfully, and seriously. A school in slum or suburb in which free writing isn't going on is a failure, whatever its reading scores.

In thinking about the school curriculum, the Collaborative's writers could profit by taking a look at a quarterly called *Foxfire*, put out by students and a teacher at the Rabun Gap-Nacoochie High School in Rabun Gap, Georgia. *Foxfire* is accurately recording Appalachian folkways, arts, crafts, and traditions. It has good book reviews, poems, and art work that seem to be mainly by adult contributors. But the heart of the *Foxfire* endeavor is an extensive series of taped interviews done by the students with mountain people, talking about crafts and traditions. One whole issue is about log-cabin building, another has pieces on quilting, chair-making, soap-making, and other trades. Another carries detailed anecdotes, notes, and photographs on hunting and training dogs; directions for dressing and cooking raccoon, 'possum, and groundhog, as well as more familiar game animals like deer. A long section explains all about slaughtering, curing, and cooking hogs. There is a splendid interview with an outspoken old lady named Aunt Arie who lives alone in a log cabin; as the students help her cook a pig's head, she describes her terror when a freezing spell swelled the door to her food cellar and she couldn't get in. There is an editorial attacking the antique dealers in the region, who sound like a pack of swindlers. One victim describes a scoundrelly free-loader right out of Mark Twain:

> But he can pray a good prayer. He comes one evenin' an' it
> come up a storm an' he got down on his knees on one side a'

th' well an' see, I can't get down on my knees, an'—got down on his knees. an' you never heared such a prayer come out'a nobody in your life as come out'a that man. An' I's standin' there about t'faint a'standin' there so long. I'd been run all day and starved t'death anyhow; an' I'uz just glad when he got done. He prayed a good prayer though. He just prayed a real good'n. He comes in about the time I got dinner ready, and he comes in an' eats.

The main point of students' writing is not the finished work, the poem or whatever, but how the experience helps students. With *Foxfire*, what clearly counts is the experience of putting it all together. Reading *Foxfire*, you sense that some students in Rabun Gap with their tape recorders and cameras are really learning something.

Street Academies: 1968

Street academies are schools run by the New York Urban League, manned by teachers and streetworkers, operating out of the abandoned storefronts that litter Harlem like empty shells on a beach. They have had considerable success in reaching dropouts (others call them pushouts) from city high schools. In two years they sent something like 140 Harlem and Lower East Side students in New York to various colleges, and more than that are now preparing for college in street academies and in two private schools linked to the program. The number of storefronts constantly changes, as does their function; in past years the tendency was to begin with a lot and then, through the course of a year, to shake down to a manageable number. Some are engaged in job training and setting youths up in local business, some in street work and recreation; there's one for young dope addicts; about ten offer formal academic instruction.

The formal program is a ladder with three rungs, the lowest being the street academy proper, a storefront serving anywhere from ten to thirty students. An academy has three teachers (with college degrees) and three streetworkers. Of the 120 workers in the New York City program, I observed in the summer of 1968, about 70 were black, mostly from Harlem; a growing number are alumni of the academies. Streetworkers usually live in the neighborhood where they work; a few maintain apartments for homeless kids. Each academy has its own atmosphere, but what is taught is roughly the same: a mixture of basic, often remedial reading and math, and subjects like African and black history, sometimes Arabic or Swahili, and sociology which usually means discussing life in Harlem.

After anywhere from six weeks to a year in a street academy, half the students graduate to the second rung of the ladder, another storefront called the Academy of Transition, which offers some systematic preparation. Then, after achieving eighth- or ninth-grade levels of performance, students are recommended for the third stage, one of two college preparatory schools, Newark Prep and Harlem Prep. (So far about nine in ten of the students in the Academy of Transition have gone on.)

A visitor's notes: streetworker watching a student squinting at a book. It turns out the boy never had his eyes examined. A few days later I notice he is wearing glasses. "Reading problem, shit," was all the worker said. Another tells of a student who always falls asleep in class; when he is examined a doctor discovers a small piece of paper stuck in his left ear. For years, nobody had noticed that he was half-deaf.

An intense young teacher, black, is delivering an impassioned lecture on slavery. Part of his text is drawn from Stanley Elkins's study; he describes the Midlle Passage, reads an account of the mutilation and murder of a slave, talks about uprisings and revolts. Later, a student came up to me and demanded to know what I thought of the lecture. I said it was fine, but it left me wondering, as historians do, why there had been so few Nat Turners. I told him about Elkins's notion that the institution of slavery had, to some degree, really turned strong men into Sambos, docile, watermelon-eating darkies. He resented this—it was a slur, white history—but he was interested, and we kept talking out on the street. He was a dropout from Benjamin Franklin High; through a streetworker, he had begun spending time at the storefront. This history was better than what they taught in school—George Washington and phony stuff —but what he liked most about the teachers here was that they asked things of you, even homework. He was scornful of school where teachers were always trying to make deals with the kids, where you could study or not, just so long as you didn't make trouble. That and the police all over the building, disguised as students, really bothered him. He attended classes here all morning; in the afternoon, he did chores in the storefront to earn Neighborhood Youth Corps money ($38 a week) and hung around talking to the workers. He was proud of the fact that his studies here were academic, college preparatory. This seemed more important to him than the promise of college, which was still vague and far away, though it would be nice to get out of Harlem and see some grass and trees for a change.

In another academy: a white teacher goes through a reader with a handful of students in a remedial class; two move along pretty well, two others don't. He explains that the kids who come in with a sixth- or seventh-grade reading level are fairly easy to bring up to high-school standards. It's a matter of getting them to read more, to find things they are interested in. But some are in bad shape, reading at second- or third-grade levels or lower, and there is so little material for them that isn't stupid or boring. He thinks the streetworkers coddle them; they have to learn to read, and all this rapping about Harlem and the state of the black soul isn't going to teach them phonics. "But a lot of them wouldn't be here without one or two of the street-workers."

I saw some reports of books a class was reading: Langston Hughes, Richard Wright, Malcolm X. The reports were competent, but not as interesting as the journals two students showed me, full of the kind of abstractly philo-sophical, yet confessional writing that people their age often do: "My existence is a mystery to me. . . ."

In the Academy of Transition: a remarkably patient older teacher goes over an algebra problem time and time again for the benefit of a puzzled youth. In the next room a young teacher reads the class a dialect poem by Robert Burns, which is to illustrate the beginning of Romanticism. The poem, "To a Mouse," is incomprehensible to many in the class and to me. In their notebooks, some duly record the main features of the impending Romantic Movement. The teacher, a little embarrassed, explains to me that there is an emphasis on contemporary works, but it's also thought that the students need to know "some of the rest of this." She is right about contemporary literature: besides black writers, students said they were reading Hemingway and Steinbeck. Down the hall, a teacher is lecturing on African history, the rise of Islam. Three of his students seem fascinated. They are Muslims, and the divisions in the faith following the death of Mohammed intrigue them. After class they explain some of the unfamiliar names to me and another student. As we talk, a voice across the way is asking what a personal pronoun is. "A person, place or thing," comes the reluctant answer. "No, a personal pronoun is. . . ."

A streetworker and a teacher lead an earnest discussion touching on hairstyles—"what no brother does to his hair" —and the older generation's skin creams and permanents, which anger many in the class. The teacher, looking about the same age as the students, attempts to balance their arguments—parents are products of different times, you have to respect the experiences they lived through—but the class isn't having any of it. At one point the teacher launches into a vehement sermon on the evils of dope. After World War II, he says, powerful teenage gangs grew up in Harlem, and the whites were so alarmed by this militance that they had introduced the narcotics trade on a large scale to break black bodies and spirits. Now again Harlem is stirring; this time they mustn't let the pushers defeat them.

In some academies, portraits of Malcolm X were in evidence; copies of his autobiography were everywhere, and I got to talking with one student about the contrast between Malcolm and King. He said he admired King, had wept when he was killed, but never felt he could be like King. Malcolm was closer; he represented qualities you yourself could aim at: richer possibilities. When a streetworker joined us, I asked about the courses in black and African history—it seemed to me that the lectures were good but I wasn't sure how much they meant; some students were fascinated, others weren't. They agreed that to many these were mainly courses to enjoy or dislike; it was easy to exaggerate students' interest in black subjects. But they both insisted there was a growing mood or racial pride and anger, and it was important that courses be given that interpreted this mood to the kids. The streetworker said that a few intensely serious students needed—he didn't want to say a religion or an ideology—but something that gave them an idea of how to interpret the world, some coherent body of ideals: "They can work out their own lives, you know, but they need a start, especially the ones going on to white colleges, because that's a hard scene." I wondered whether African history or even the personal example of a militant streetworker would lead to a coherent body of black ideals. He wasn't sure; nor did he know if a school could offer what he was talking about as well as, say, a Muslim organization. At its best, black consciousness could be a channel for hopes and angers; it could prepare students for what would be a lifelong struggle; and maybe a feeling of black solidarity could make it easier to grapple with the white world. It might also serve to counter the dog-eat-dog individualism of the streets. For some, he admitted, the upshot would be fanaticism and black jingoism. We ended talking about the great difference between playing the role of a black and actually achieving an *identity;* playing a role you are still dancing on somebody else's string, whereas an identity is something you forge for yourself.

One of the strengths (and oddities) of the street academy program is the incongruous collection of people it has assembled. Representatives of very different kinds of past and present efforts to reach people in Harlem coexist and overlap, like geological strata. There are white seminarians and university students, Muslims, black nationalists, and people of more respectable cut who prefer to call themselves Negroes. The man who started and still runs the program, a white former streetworker named Harv Oostdyk, was once connected with a suburban Christian movement called Young Life. He began some years ago with a tutorial center for dropouts in the Church of the Master on Morningside Avenue, and a number of his original recruits were also Young Lifers: some are still on the staff. "Harv has learned a lot," a black worker said. "Used to be every other word was Jesus, but Jesus hasn't all that much of a following in Harlem, and now he's stopped that kind of talk." Oostdyk continues nonetheless to speak in tones reminiscent of muscular Christianity and ruggedly individualistic uplift. He talks of the need for streetworkers with "charisma," capable of "hand-to-hand combat" to save kids from the streets. He has a vision of great corporate involvement in the renewal of the ghetto, arguing that business is the one segment of white society black people do not regard with disillusionment.

Some of the former Young Lifers and some of the black streetworkers share what sometimes seems a *mystique* of streetwork: "These kids are looking for answers, and we have them." Others describe their roles more modestly. Some see themselves as teachers, some as accomplices of the kids against the system, giving them practical skills by which they can survive and fight back. Some say their main contribution is simply to demonstrate by their existence alternatives to dope, hustling, or dead-end jobs. One white streetworker worried about his own lack of training: youngsters with smashed lives, real victims of Harlem, often need professional help, and he isn't in a position to give any. A black worker who mistrusted words like *charisma* and *motivation* described what he does this way: "I'm available; the kids know I'm like them. Some can take a lesson. Any kid who's been able to keep from getting all strung up, who's able to move on up, is strong to begin with. This program is finding the strong and helping them, otherwise it's kidding itself." Some workers are conservative, scornful of activists they see as Harlem "community" spokesmen without a community, militant leaders without followers: "I try to teach self-help and not a lot of crap about a revolution that isn't going to happen." Others regard themselves as black revolutionaries in some sense. Joking, I asked one of these how it felt to be a revolutionary working for the Urban

League. He answered, seriously, that he does worry that the
program might just be the system putting its best foot for-
ward. Its premises are basically individualistic: although
some of the kids will return later to work in the ghetto, it
is hard to be confident they will, hard not to suspect it is
taking leadership out of Harlem. But he wasn't sure. The
scene at colleges these days was so different: it was easier
to stay black and angry. "When you see what happens to
all the talent here, you want to cry. Then you want to do
something about it." Another, a "nationalist," had fewer
doubts: "If there were a revolution tomorrow, you'd still
need storefronts like these to reach the kids." Both made a
very odd contrast to Allah, the leader of a Muslim Splinter
group called the Five Percenters, the "righteous Teachers."
The Five Percenters operate an academy still loosely linked
to the program, although there are few regular academic
classes there now, and Allah complained of neglect. In his
view "the children" need more training for jobs and literacy; only a few could take advantage of college preparatory
courses, and without basic skills they were going to fall
prey to "savages and wolves in the streets."

The streetworkers are young; they get $6,000 a year,
and despite the prestige of the job—many students I talked
to said they'd like to do streetwork—I didn't suppose most
would stay with it for more than four or five years. I put
this to one worker, and he said this was a fair assumption.
What would they do later? Some would end up as poverty
bureaucrats, wheeling and dealing in the maze of agencies
in the city. If the schools and other institutions ever
opened up to new sources of talent, some would want to
keep working with kids or teaching. A few might make it
into politics, building from a base in the streets. What kind
of politics was anybody's guess. In conversations like these,
people alternated between a guess that, after all, nothing

would ever change in the ghetto and hunches that Harlem, and particularly young Harlem, is up for grabs.

No single group in the program—whites, blacks, militants, moderates—had a monopoly on good teaching or good streetwork. What the effective people did seem to share was a quality I first thought of as moralism and later came to think of as moral passion. There were no *laissez-faire* teachers: the good ones preached, made demands, and seemed to indicate that learning is a serious business. My impression was that the effective whites emphasized making something of yourself to the students, while the blacks, especially the more militant, put more stress on communal identity. The whites, when they seemed to strike false notes, did so on the side of sanctimoniousness, the corresponding black temptation being a sort of showy bogusness.

Anyone who sets out to help the children of the poor into college has come to terms with the fact that there is a system in our educational institutions, an interlocking set of material, cultural, and psychological barriers that separate out those who succeed from those who don't. This is a truism, as it is a truism to say that the system is based on ignoring many vital differences between students—the rates at which they learn, their separate interests. The street academies have, to an extent, broken out of the usual standardizations imposed by the schools. Partly they do this by what they teach—though not, it must be said, by their methods of teaching, which are strictly conventional. The African and black history, the self-conscious militance of some of the teachers and workers do have an appeal. And, in part, the academies break the mold by where they are—on the streets—and by first connecting with kids through streetworkers before trying to teach them anything. It makes a world of difference that they, unlike the schools, deal with willing volunteers.

It would be a mistake to ignore the hunger of many of the dropouts in the program for manageable challenges—even conventional ones of the sort that schools are routinely supposed to offer. Personal pronouns and a sketchy sense of the relation of Burns to the Romantic Movement do not seem to me particularly worth mastering. But to a few earnest youngsters returning to give learning a last chance, they are steps on the road to education, and are thus taken seriously. The faith in education that endures beneath layers of cynicism and despair after years of contact with the schools is mysterious, touching, and in some respects a little alarming; it makes these young people seem awfully vulnerable. In some academies you see lists of rules —no swearing, no hats—which students have agreed to and in some cases have drawn up. This is part of what many are looking for, though vain efforts at enforcing the same rules absorb almost all the energies of teachers and administrators in conventional schools.

The academies are far from being oppressive places; unlike the schools, there is considerable coming and going and cheerful noise. Yet a visitor leaves with a puzzling impression that there is little difference between many aspects of their working and the way an ordinary principal would want his high school to function. (Somehow this makes the failure of the city high schools seem all the worse.) Since the academies are trying to teach students how to beat a system, they are required to make substantial concessions to it. A major concession is the stress on preparation for college, which turns out to be more complicated than it looks at first sight.

Most obviously, there is the shameful waste of talent in Harlem, where half the students drop out of high school, and three-fourths of those who remain settle for the general diploma. The street academies are proving that some of the dropouts, if reached, can be pointed toward college. The will to achieve is strong among at least a part of the new generation in the ghettos. This is putting a tremendous strain on all institutions which have failed them, not just the schools; but the schools face unprecedented demands to help lift students out of the submerged classes. The notion is spreading among the ambitious young in the ghetto that college is one of the few legitimate paths out. To a startling extent, the new ghetto generation has adopted the increasingly meritocratic assumptions of the rest of America, its preoccupation with degrees and credentials. There is suspicion that very few jobs offered black people without college degrees are in any sense a man's work. We see, too, in these street academies a reflection of the experience of many students with the urban high schools. As whites flee the cities, these schools become less and less concerned with college preparation. Nothing they do suggests to students that they are worthy enough to consider college a real option. The classes taught for the general diploma are essentially custodial in nature; employers take a dim view of the diploma anyway, and what is taught is not worth learning. This has led to a situation where even students who drop out retain some respect for the idea of academic (college-preparatory) courses, however badly taught or irrelevant to their day-to-day concerns. They think of them, rightly or wrongly, as equipping them with skills that will lead somewhere. More important, they offer a token of something vital to the educational process: an assurance that the school considers them worth teaching. There are absurdities in the situation: in a sense, meritocratic America is being threatened by the power of its own symbols. But it exists. For more and more ghetto students, dropouts or not, it is an academic course or nothing.

Someone once told me that years ago a New York

school conducted an experiment which amounted to little more than urging every student to go to college. Outsiders came in and explained that scholarships and loans were possible, and the school promised to give students special help and keep in touch with them when they went away. By itself this improved academic performance, and led to less truancy, higher IQs, and so on. Something similar is at work in the academies. Plenty of academy students can give you straightforward reasons for being there. They tell you it's because they want a crack at better jobs and a decent existence, a chance to move up and out of Harlem. One rather sour worker told me: "They're taught to hustle real early. Some of them think college is the new hustle. To them a degree is like a big car." Some are drawn to the program, at least at first, by the Youth Corps salaries a number of students receive as work-scholarships. But for others, the storefronts and the workers present a challenge to make something of themselves. The fact that the medium of the challenge is a college-preparatory course is secondary. The academies offer a sense that what you learn might carry you to a real future in which there are choices although the achievements along the way are not always convincing or intrinsically worthwhile. Any solid identity, we are told, depends on feeling that one has such choices.

It is no reflection on the academies to point out that only some of their students are able to proceed to the preparatory schools and then college. The aspirations of the remainder have been taken seriously. (This is something, but not, obviously, enough.) One student said his reading wasn't so good. He was making progress, because here they tried to help you find out what was wrong, and didn't give you tests to flunk you. I asked him about colleges, and he looked uncomfortable. His friends had made fun of him for trying to get into the army; he was disappointed when he failed part of the written exam. What he wanted to do was to be a gunsmith. He knew all about guns. The academy was a good place to him, it was trying to set up job training courses and local businesses, but he wasn't really being helped. Talking to him made me reflect again on the depressing quality of life in a society that so inadequately enlists the diverse talents and imagination of its youth.

Newark and Harlem Prep, which take the academies' graduates, are dissimilar institutions. Newark Prep is a sixty-year-old private school that began by taking a few of Oostdyk's tutees and now fills a majority—around eighty—of its places with academy students bused daily from Harlem. In 1968, it placed twenty seven academy students in college. Its white headmaster, Daniel Alvino, is the compleat private school principal, cheerful, much taken up with rules—recently he has relaxed on beards and dress—college-board scores, and the shocking state of the transcripts that come from the Harlem public schools. Classes are quite formal, the curriculum is that of the standard private school. The students return from this universe to Harlem in the afternoon to tutor younger kids in the Academy of Transition, or get help for themselves, or just to hang around with the workers and teachers. "Newark Prep is like out in the world," a student said. "Straight and kind of up-tight, not like the academy. It tells you what to expect."

Harlem Prep, an institution spun off from the academy program and no longer linked directly to it, finished its first year in 1968. It raises its own money, mostly from smaller foundations in New York. Most of its seventy students are academy graduates. It placed thirty students in college in 1968. During the winter it is housed in a cavernous old armory near the Harlem River Drive; the summer session I visited was out on the shady campus of another private school. Edward Carpenter, its black headmaster, and a circle of students were seated around a lunch table; colleges were being discussed. Recruiters from Brandeis had been around, and two students were thinking about going there. The talk drifted to politics and the future of the races. Mr. Carpenter had told me that he was strictly apolitical, that the school had to stay clear of "that New York jungle" to remain independent, and I was curious what he would say. A student in Muslim dress said the only answer was a fifty-first state, a black people's state where they could control their own lives. This was met with scorn by another who said that revolution was the only answer. A girl wondered whether you could have a revolution in economics and politics without violence, and this was denied by another student who said that nothing was achieved without at least the threat of violence. This student thought a political alliance of blacks and discontented whites was possible. Through all this, Mr. Carpenter was the pedagogue. He would accept a premise and then urge the speaker to develop a program from it: how would you work the problem of the black people who didn't want to move to the fifty-first state? what institutions would a revolution develop? what alliances were possible with whites? and what if whites took up the challenge of violence and counter-challenged? He was mainly interested in getting them to develop their arguments, which they did with vigor. It impressed me as an honest job of teaching. He did not condescend to the students by automatically accepting their fashionable militance; on the other hand he took what they said seriously, as indeed anyone in these days should.

He invited me to visit his math class, but it was hot, and I opted for a cooler room, a tiny English class. Two students were doing a kind of recitation, delivering a five-minute talk and then responding to questions and criticisms. The first student talked in loose terms about America as a racist society, and the floor gave him rather a hard time, asking him to explain what he meant or to prove various assertions. Another student began to play the role of a white critic, raising all the standard arguments in favor of racism and the status quo but elaborating on them in an extremely skillful way, obviously deriving a good deal of sardonic pleasure from his act. Then a second student delivered his recitation, a meditative set of questions on existence of the kind I had heard in the academies, and, since there was little to do but think about them, the teacher passed around two poems on jazz which were read and discussed intelligently.

An English teacher, white, told me that his students were a mixed lot; all were pretty good. Some were at Harlem Prep simply to better themselves, whereas a growing number were more hip, more socially conscious and aware. He wondered whether there was a black version of the growing white upper-middle-class social concern. The brighter black students were much more militant, he said. I wondered whether part of this might not come from their mistrust of their own ability to withstand the lures of life at a white university: there was a tone of worried defiance during the lunchtable discussion. This may have only indicated that the students realized how awesome a jump they were going to have to make from Harlem to a white campus.

Mother Dowd, a nun in charge of Harlem Prep's relations with colleges, said it was too early to say anything about how graduates were faring at different colleges— NYU, Fordham, Wesleyan, or various schools within the New York state system. She had a certain amount of experience placing black students, and she rather thought that these *were* better prepared psychologically, but there would, in any case, be a certain amount of anguish. One group of five at the University of Buffalo that summer session had constituted themselves as a militant black student caucus separate from the existing black students' group. But militance did not take you very far unless your academic preparation was good. I asked whether students from Newark and Harlem Prep would be able to thrive in a conventional college program. She thought they had the training (it seemed so to me) but that really boring programs and unsympathetic teachers might disillusion them. She hoped that such students could prompt colleges to improve their wretched teaching.

We talked about the future of the academies—how far they could expand, the extent to which they could replace the ghetto high schools. My feeling was that most universities are only ready to do a limited amount for the children of the poor. Christopher Jencks and David Riesman have explained why colleges are unlikely to expand programs to include poor students—almost every institutional pressure and status badge in the university system inclines administrators to prefer able students who conform to standard programs, over needy students who might not fit in.* Still, as Mother Dowd pointed out, there are many more places now in colleges than there are black applicants.

The entire academy program is shifting toward more involvement with the public schools, and particularly Benjamin Franklin High. A distinct college preparatory wing inside Benjamin Franklin High School has been established, with eighty graduates of street academies. (Where this will leave Newark and Harlem Prep is not altogether clear. Both expect to have street academy alumni next year; Newark Prep already has its own sources of students, and Harlem

*See *Academic Revolution* by Christopher Jencks and David Riesman, Doubleday, 1968.

Prep is widening its admissions nets, too.) Dropouts and truants from Benjamin Franklin will be farmed out to ten street academies, where streetworkers and teachers will prepare them to return to the "Prep Wing." The program is now negotiating on such key matters as the selection of teachers. There are plans for starting programs in other high schools.

At the start, the bulk of the money to finance the academies has come from the Ford Foundation ($700,000) with some funds coming from the Neighborhood Youth Corps and the city. Mr. Oostdyk has persuaded a number of companies—including IBM, the First National City Bank, Celanese, and others—each to sponsor an academy in the Franklin complex. (A large academy costs about $50,000 a year to run.) In a series of complicated moves, he has tied the academies to a city program of neighborhood "satellites," smaller storefronts for streetwork and recreation.

The street academy staff is ambitious (though already spread too thin), and the new arrangements will make financing less chancy. But there are grounds for concern. The street academies have succeeded because they have worked from the streets up. First they established contact with students through streetworkers and teachers, then adapted the institutions to fit what grew out of this relationship. They were truly decentralized units—small and with a fair amount of autonomy for teachers and workers. This enabled them to assemble radically different sorts of people. Such an approach stands in direct contrast to the kind of grandiose institutional engineering the foundations like to sponsor in the name of "fundamental change." It runs counter to the ethos of both schools and large corporations.

The price of involvement with public schools and corporations may, in the end, be too high. There will certainly be troubles involved in keeping the present assortment of people. Already one academy has been closed because its director was thought too extreme, and the Five Percenter Academy is being allowed to languish. The program needs to be as various as the streets, and yet it is hard to envision militant streetworkers toeing a line chalked by the city schools, just as it is hard to believe that many corporate officials would be pleased by the tone of some of the discussions I heard.

The more the program ties in with the schools, the more it will have to reconsider its narrow aims. It is one thing to run street academies aiming to persuade gifted dropouts to go to college; it is quite another to set up an elite program in one part of a dispirited, mutinous city high school. The street academies will have to begin thinking of other challenges besides college to offer the mass of angry black youth in the cities.

Two Community Schools: Boston, 1968

The New School for Children in Boston occupies a cheerful, cluttered building across the street from a public school that looks like the prison ship in *Great Expectations*; it has ninety children, kindergarten through the fifth grade. The Community School has, at the moment, settled its forty nine children—kindergarten through second grade—in a cramped maze of small rooms in the basement of St. Ann's Episcopal Church. Both are examples of a new kind of school—independent private schools set up by parents in the ghetto. Both began in 1967 and are showing a tenacious ability to endure in the face of steep odds. Each is a variation on a theme, community schooling, and each is thus a separate, uncompleted essay in definition of elusive words like *community* and *participation*.

They have common roots, for at the outset there was only one group of Roxbury people interested in starting an independent school. Mostly black, but with some whites, it formed in a mood of desperation after Louise Day Hicks's sweep of the 1965 Boston school-board election. Some were associated in one way or another with the tutorial program run out of St. Ann's. Most were parents who had come to distrust the public schools, and although they disagreed on many points, they were united in wanting a school that could be depended upon not to cripple their kids; that was the minimum. Some wanted the feeling of being able to shape at least part of their children's future; a few had a specific interest in seeing their children placed in informal classes, where they could work at their own level and in their own time.

The division into two groups reflected a faint division along class and neighborhood lines. What became the Community School group had markedly more "certifiable poor"—people whose income falls below official poverty levels—most of them clustered in the framehouse apartments around St. Ann's. What became the New School group had more people whose incomes are middling, more whites, more people from the general Roxbury area. The Community School operates without tuition; the New School charges $250 a year, granting scholarships to its needy children.

One point of contention between the groups was the degree to which a good school in the ghetto needs outside help. Obviously outside money was needed; but to what extent could a school go it alone? The New School enthusiasts wanted a crack school for their children, and they were eager, or at least willing, to enlist the support of schools of education in the Boston area and educational experts of one kind or another, as well as the energies of various prominent Roxbury figures. This bent was reinforced by the principal, Mrs. Bernice Miller, a former Chicago school principal who believed that the New School would have to go beyond its own circle to draw on a wide base of support if it was to flourish as a model enterprise. The Community School people, on the other hand, were interested in having a good school, but they wanted the school to be *theirs*: they were suspicious of the amount of outside involvement in the New School. They were also wary of administrators and decided to call their principal simply the head teacher. (The first head teacher was Mrs. Doreen Wilkinson, a lovely black lady with a good deal of sympathy for the parents' outlook.) Both schools have tried to set up a network of Friends of the School for raising money in fairly small sums in Boston and the suburbs. So far they seem to have made this precarious financing work, but as each plans to add a grade a year, budgets will grow and fund-raising will become tougher.

There is no rivalry between the two schools; they are simply not the same. The New School has come to identify with Roxbury as a whole. Its wider base of support and its ability to appeal to many different interests have made it a community venture in a broad, almost political sense—the sense that Roxbury Negroes use when, prematurely and not always accurately, they speak of themselves as a black community. It has become one of the symbols of Roxbury's aspirations and draws on the support of people sympathetic to those aspirations—progressive educators, liberal suburbanites, as well as private schools like Shady Hill. Classes are informal, the atmosphere is lively and warm. (Kids come and sit on a visitor's lap.) There's a tendency toward the faddishness you see in the rare, self-consciously experimental suburban school, but so far it has been checked by the extraordinary quality of two former Boston school teachers who took the first and second grades.

The Community School defines its community differently. The center of it is the parents, most of whom live near St. Ann's. (The school has a loan to renovate part of a nearby house, which in time it will move to.) There are a few outsiders on its board; the school is largely a neighborhood affair. Here, too, classes are informal, although maneuvering ir tiny basement rooms puts a strain on teachers and children. There are three teachers and two assistant teachers, ladies from the neighborhood. (At the New School parents work in the office and in a variety of other ways, but they don't teach.)

I could not argue, in the language of the social scientists dominating our educational discourse, that these two schools are models or even hypotheses. What they prove is still being worked out, assuming that the wild tangle of variables we call a school can ever be said to have proved anything. They testify to a fierce desire on the part of ordinary people to develop workable alternatives to public education. They show that ghetto parents will approve of informal classes quite unlike anything they had when they were in school. (One lady, however, said she liked the informal classes because they reminded her of the one-room schoolhouse she attended as a girl in rural Alabama.) Community schools seem to be spreading, despite the absence of any workable means of financing them. They may represent a Children's Crusade, or they may, after all, only be telling everybody a simple lesson about educational reform: don't wait to work out theories of what community participation means; certainly don't wait for guarantees about money. Begin a school, do good work on a small, manageable scale, and perhaps reality will catch up to you. If there are enough such enterprises, learned men will be set to devising ways that their existence can be made to square with common sense, public finance, and all that. In the meantime, they exist, they teach live children; that's miracle enough to stagger the experts.

Career Ladders for Poor People

The Talent Corps—"A College for Human Services"—was started by a handful of reformist middle-class ladies with the idea of training poor women for jobs as assistants to professionals in what are called the human services: schools, hospitals, and other social agencies in New York City. Not a terribly radical idea, you would say. Yet as it evolves into a two-year institution of higher learning, the Talent Corps is cutting more and more against the grain of our educational order.

The Talent Corps is a refinement of some ideas that have been in the air since the early sixties, when America began to rediscover poverty and a number of theorists—I suppose the first was the sociologist Frank Riessman—proposed creating new careers for the poor by setting up permanent jobs in various understaffed human services areas of the economy, jobs that would include career ladders, on-the-job training allowing able poor people to rise to professional positions. Thus, the theory ran, we would provide decent work for many and improve services while reducing the level of warfare between professionals and the poor neighborhoods they supposedly serve.

The new-careers theorists subsequently have managed to touch on various absurdities in the organization of American life. They note the massive shortages of hands in the service sectors of the economy. They say, with justice, that present vocational programs are a costly disaster, equipping people for obsolete jobs—like the unhappy students I saw in a Boston high school, sitting on the asphalt studying agriculture. The proponents of new careers raise questions about our entire system of licensing and credentialing professionals. It makes little sense to demand four years of an academic high-school program and a lengthy, specialized college and graduate school training to produce a preschool teacher or a streetworker. It is obvious that many service jobs require qualities—an ability to learn from practical experience, patience, kindliness, responsiveness—that no graduate school has yet been able to incorporate into its curriculum. Such jobs could probably be filled by poor people who lack the prescribed credentials, if only there were alternatives to the existing meritocratic entryways.

All this is so, and yet, with some exceptions, the career programs have not been as successful as their originators hoped. Plenty of new jobs have resulted—some 300,000 people are working as paraprofessionals in public schools, programs sponsored by the Office of Economic Opportunity or hospitals and health services around the country—but many of the jobs are still wretched and badly paid dead ends. Federal and big-city authorities have filled entire file cases with paper career ladders which, as matters stand, few living souls will ever climb.

Although they have gained some footholds and are organizing to gain more—in groups like the National Association of New Careerists—the new-careers advocates are still scratching at the surfaces of the system's walls. The lack of progress is not hard to understand. It is an ancient guild-union rule, understood throughout the ages by all professions, that restricted entry increases the power and earnings of the brotherhood. This rule has been extended absurdly by professional groups in America into areas like social work and medicine where it would seem to an outsider that shortages of trained people are a perpetual problem. Also, the notion of making room for bottom dogs flies in the face of one of the unstated functions of the educational system, which is to act as a social sieve separating those who get ahead from those who don't. Then, too, training professionals on the job, emphasizing performance rather than credentials, disrupts the lines of gravitational force exerted by the graduate school which have succeeded in refashioning college teaching in their own professional image —virtually killing off older notions of liberal-arts education in the process—and are now altering the shape of high-school education as well. Thus, working against any expansion of the new-careers movement is a powerful combination of class and institutional interests plus one of the greatest of social forces, inertia. As despairing social critics have noted, these processes are at work everywhere. They are nationally standardized, like methods for stamping out sheet metal.

The immense, stifling uniformity is certainly intimidating. There are, however, forces running in another direction whose strength is hard to gauge. We know there is a crisis in public services in our cities, among whose myriad causes is a shortage of professional help. At the lower levels of the public service hierarchies, at least, new people can be absorbed without threatening existing jobholders. We know that high schools and colleges have largely failed to open up real alternatives to the academic grind; for more and more children of the affluent, as well as many children of the poor, the curriculum is, in the vague and well-worn phrase, irrelevant. Genuinely educational work-study alternatives would be welcome, but the high schools and colleges are atrophied and unable to respond. Within certain of the multiversities, there are soft stirrings in work-study directions. New interests and forces are emerging. Teachers' unions and professional groups are demanding more control over entry and promotions, which are still in the hands of what often looks like a conspiracy between the school managers and the teachers colleges. They see that one way to break this hold and win more influence for

teachers would be to make training more clinical—centered
in schools and classrooms—than it currently is. In education
and elsewhere, some of the new public service unions are
eager to organize and represent paraprofessionals. In New.
York, for example, both District Council 37 of the state
and municipal workers' union, and the United Federation
of Teachers have been busy organizing; District Council 37
has devised an interesting plan for hospital assistants to
train on the job and qualify as practical nurses. Some
of the concern for new careers on the part of the unions reflects rosy anticipation of the day when demands for re-
leased study time, university credit for on-job training, and
educational sabbaticals will be discussed at bargaining
tables. The future of new careers in the cities is likewise
bound up with the future of the struggle for community
control, and with more lay participation in schools and
other public institutions. One aspect of the community
control tangle is the drive for more jobs and professional
openings for blacks and Puerto Ricans. There is, thus, a
constituency for new-careers programs. If an accord is ever
reached between professional groups and ghetto residents,
one clause in the peace treaty may be many more career
ladders for local people.

But if new-careers programs are to spread, they will
still have to overcome a good many obstacles. To under-
state the matter ludicrously, our public service bureaucracies are not accustomed to enhancing the potential of the
people in them, particularly those on the bottom—who in
the hospitals get the dirty work and in the schools end up
spending their time licking envelopes. Leaving aside racial
issues—which can never really be left aside—administrators
are frequently too busy to cooperate with training programs. When they have the time, even with the best will in
the world, they often don't know how; they aren't used to

thinking of themselves as educators nor of jobs as places where people learn. Another bureaucratic dilemma is that new careers programs are usually negotiated into existence by mutually suspicious agencies in an atmosphere heavy with empire-building and buck-passing. It is often far from clear who has responsiblity for making work a learning experience. Nobody is in charge, a state of affairs that may be meat and drink to some veterans of civil service treadmills, but which makes it hard for a program to maintain a direction. More or less by default, everyone has recourse to the contemporary American response to all social problems: they turn responsibility for training over to local universities or junior colleges which are, as a rule, unprepared to give practical training and not adept at reaching people who have little education. This fact—that most universities aren't good at giving practical training—is rediscovered daily as the universities are pushed and tempted into doing more and more of the work of other failing institutions. For years, graduates of teachers' colleges have been pointing out that universities can't teach you how to teach. There are exceptions: a few junior colleges and universities are setting up truly clinical and inductive programs; in general, though, the world of academic credits and the world of jobs and services are hard to mesh.

Another problem for new careers is the relationship with students. Intelligently relating study to work is hard enough, but when middle-class professionals face poor and black students, there are the usual misunderstandings, suspicion, and racism. People who have met failure in schools and jobs are bitter and anxious—they need sustained encouragement. This is awkwardly related to a final perplexity of the new careers programs: the difficulty in screening out unpromising people. They begin with a laudable desire to get away from the usual corrupting standards of high-school diplomas and the even less reliable filters of class and racial perceptions, which give the advantage to the scrubbed candidate with the yassuh manners. Still, it does not stand to reason that everybody will be equally good at, say, lay therapy with drug addicts. In the absence of those supposedly hard, objective standards so prevalent in America and in their fear of expressing bias, those in charge of new-careers programs are reluctant to make personal judgments as to which applicants are more suitable. If they had more time, money, and a wider margin for mistakes, they might be able to devise sensible procedures for matching candidates to jobs; but usually they don't.

The Talent Corps, which has operated in several forms since 1964—it started out only admitting women and was called the Women's Talent Corps—has confronted many of these problems. It is remarkable first because of the quality of what it does—a good place for learning is always rare and worth noting—and second because it is evolving in ways that set it apart from most new-careers programs. Now it is in the process of becoming a "College for Human Services" with a charter from New York State to grant its students two-year junior college degrees. This may seem like small beer, but in a world of oppressive institutional sameness, the Corps has within it a germ of hope that higher education can be reformed.

The students it admits are adults (still mostly women) between the ages of twenty one and sixty. Half are on welfare at the beginning of their training, eighty percent are black and fifteen percent Puerto Rican, the remainder being Chinese or white. Most have families; a third have four or more children to take care of when they go home in the evening. There are more applicants than places—in 1968, 2,500 for 200 places. (Many are rejected because their income exceeds the levels of certifiable poverty set by the

U.S. Department of Labor which pays for much of the Talent Corps operation—$3,200 yearly income for a family of four.) Students are chosen on the basis of simple written tests and interviews. The tests are not stiff—reading and writing ability at something like a sixth- to an eighth-grade level: about half of the Talent Corps students have high-school degrees. What the interviewers say they look for is elusive—interest, eagerness, social concern. In practice final selection depends on whether there are openings of on-the-job training in an applicant's neighborhood.

The curriculum combines work and study—three days of work in a school, hospital, or whatever alternating with two days of classes at the Talent Corps. The classes make considerable demands on students, for the premise—not common in ordinary job-training programs—is that poor adults from the ghetto want to learn theoretical and academic subjects as well as the basic skills necessary to make their way in the credentialing economy. A core curriculum is taken by everybody in the first year. It resembles some of the better "problems" courses in colleges and occasional high schools—some psychology, readings in education, and a heavy dose of sociology and social issues, particularly ghetto issues. In some of the classes I watched, for example, groups of students were preparing surveys of police and health services in different small communities they had chosen. (One group studied suburban White Plains and was surprised to find slums.) In theory the academic work is related to experiences drawn from students' job experiences, and in practice this does sometimes happen. Some of the best discussions I heard arose from field-work situations, hospital trainees explaining defects in the hospital services, swapping horror stories.

We never know exactly what students get from any course of study, but some I spoke to had carried away

ideas to digest, and were glad enough to talk about them
with various degrees of self-consciousness. One shrewd lady,
whose field work was in the schools, had studied Montessori, *Summerhill*, and a number of other works and then
had gone around to private schools in the city to check up
on the differences in practice. She had a good eye for
fraud, and was amusing on the shapes into which educational ideas are twisted. In general, psychology seemed to
click with the students, and as I listened to two of them I
tried to remember something I had heard a teacher say
once about why he preferred teaching adults: he was impressed by the hunger for interpreting past experiences that
mature students bring to a class, and also by their conviction—as people who had missed an education the first time
around—that knowledge is important. The chief impression
a visitor to the Talent Corps carries away is, once again, of
the variety of students and their incredibly different levels
and interests. (Some students notice this, too, and have
asked for grouping in some classes.)

The curriculum seems to work, although the idea of a
set curriculum always rubs me the wrong way. If I had my
druthers about the Talent Corps, there would be less of the
core and more options for students to pursue their own
interests. Yet there is a point, as well as a John Dewey-ish
earnestness to all this community study—the students are
thinking about their work—and in practice it's attractive.
Some of the earnest tone comes through in two quotes
from students' papers I read. The first is: "In a democratic
society we believe in the extra-ordinary possibilities of ordinary people." The other is from a report that captures the
more sardonic view of some of the trainees in city agencies:

> The buildings which they have chosen to bypass are the ones
> that make this area blighted. They are mostly located in the
> northern half of this area, which is actually the end of the

well-known area, Bedford-Stuyvesant. In five years, this portion of the area will be like the heart of Bedford-Stuyvesant, and the southern half will be well on its way. It appears to me that the city must have a slum, and it's now preparing Crown Heights to fill Bed-Stuy's shoes.

The teachers here, unlike those in so many places, are engaged in teaching a curriculum they helped design; with general backgrounds in teaching and social work, they are not mired in the silliness of drawing distinctions between themselves and their knowledge and the students and their ignorance. (In the second year, where the academic program consists of courses without a core program, more of the teachers are university people, who are popular.)

Nonetheless, the content of the curriculum is secondary. What seems to be going on most often is teaching at a fundamental level. I don't mean basic skills in reading and writing, although there is plenty of that, too, and it's needed—but things that poor people might have missed out on, note-taking, interviewing, filling our forms, writing simple reports, how to take part in a class discussion. (I mentioned this last to one lady, and she laughed, "Yeah, that's right. You got to know the game.") There's a lot of role-playing and in the community studies the students—including shy and soft-spoken Puerto Rican ladies—have to go out and talk to policemen and hospital officials, poll people in the street, do surveys and handle simple problems of sampling, speak up bravely enough on the telephone to get an appointment. There are hundreds of small things to do, each of which is not all that difficult, and that, I guess, is part of the point. At times it seems tedious and you wonder whether students are gaining confidence. The answer is that most are and some aren't, just as some teachers are better at pulling it off than others, for whom it looks like dull busywork.

Trainees are assigned to field work throughout the city. Of the 210 first-year students, the biggest group is in the New York schools, the next largest is in hospitals and health services, with the rest scattered throughout some thirty-odd agencies. The Talent Corps, like other new-careers programs, is vulnerable to the agencies whose placements it needs, for while it controls the academic setting, it cannot control what happens on the job. A particular set of teachers, called field coordinators, is responsible for supervising both class work and field work for small groups of around ten students. The coordinators go out to the agencies, set up the definitions of the training jobs and try to ride herd on students' supervisors in the field, but there are limits on how much they can accomplish. As it places more and more people successfully, the Talent Corps establishes contacts and acquires something of a reputation. This is strength of a kind, but it still plays from weakness much of the time.

Take the schools, for example. One of the Talent Corps' greatest coups came about as the result of lengthy negotiations between Audrey Cohen, its superb executive director, and the New York school system: the system agreed to offer poor people—among them Talent Corps trainees—a program that could, theoretically, carry them upward from the rank of teachers' assistant to the rank of teacher. The concession was small—only 1,200 places for the whole city—but the principle of the career ladder was established. There were, however, catches, and each new catch meant a new round of negotiations. It turned out that only a rare school administrator has sufficient elbow room to be able to increase the responsibilities of trainees as they moved from step to step up the ladder. And, despite all sorts of assurances, people couldn't move out of the bottom slots without first acquiring a high-school diploma; and you couldn't get very far above that without the equivalent of two years in college. These are severe demands on working people with families. To get a diploma, you either had to take the two-day equivalency exam, which scares off capable candidates, particularly the math part which is too hard; or you could attend night schools, which are exhausting, boring, and often frozen into the formulas of high-school academic programs. Ultimately, Mrs. Cohen got the system to waive the high-school diploma requirement for her graduates. Now one problem is that the rates of pay at the bottom are too low to support a family, particularly as the school system kept losing the paychecks of teaching assistants and aides.

From talks with the teaching trainees, it seemed to me that in the schools, as in other agencies, the quality of the experience depended on the supervision. Most of the teachers in schools with which the Talent Corps works are eager to get assistants, but occasionally a school will signal its distrust and fear of employing the natives—like the school that wouldn't give assistants keys to lockers or classrooms. I read part of a field report that may have been typical of some of the bad experiences of the trainees who pick lemons:

> [The teacher] had several conversations with Mrs. G. [the trainee] in which she said that this idea of creating jobs for Negroes was bad, that Negroes should earn their equality by being better than white people. She refused to call her anything but "aide," and she didn't give Mrs. G. any work to do. Mrs. G. handled the situation very well. . . . She created her own work by looking for opportunities. She listened carefully to the lessons [the teacher] taught and watched the children closely to see how well they understood. . . . She also created the kind of relationship with the children that made them approach her with problems they couldn't solve. So she created her own small group. . . .

The trainees are good, the education they are getting is

good, the problem is to join study and work, to get places in which people can learn as they work. This seems simple, but it isn't.

CHAPTER 4

...AND BAD

Northeast High

Most students at Northeast High in Philadelphia are middle class, clean, respectful, and go on to college; many win scholarships. Few are black. Northeast is the sort of school that many parents and school officials want. Frederick Wiseman's remarkable documentary film portrait of Northeast High, *High School*, shows that our most serious educational problems aren't only in slum schools. What people think of as good schools are failing their children, too.

In words alone, *High School*'s message can be reduced to a string of clichés: the schools are authoritarian, repres-

149

sive, inhuman. On film—on this film, anyway—the clichés take on density; *High School* carries us beyond slogans into artistic truth. Scene after scene builds to a powerful cumulative effect—not of anger, but of immense sadness and futility: this is how we live. *High School* is an essay on emptiness.

The camera eye is not cruel. Teachers are decent and well-meaning. What they do and say doesn't matter as much as the numbing lessons the whole institution is teaching its students about themselves and life. A school official prowls the halls, constantly checking on students to see if they have passes, harassing them as they try to talk on the telephone. Here, as in other disciplinary matters, the rule is made explicit: "Don't you talk. You just listen." In an extraordinary scene, a burly dean of discipline badgers a boy who thinks his teacher is punishing him unfairly and is resisting on principle:

> When you are being addressed by someone older than you or in a seat of authority, it's your job to respect and listen. She didn't ask you to jump from the Empire State Building .... What you should have done is showed some character .... We are out to establish that you can be a man and that you can take orders.

The sociologist Edward Shils has said that the cultural battle in our time is between the new sense of individuality and personal expressiveness that flows from a wide experience of affluence and the more traditional sense that life is lived in scarcity. The children of plentitude often, I think, fail to understand the limits of human possibilities, especially institutional possibilities. But one doesn't have to be a proponent of total liberation to see that Northeast High is preaching an ugly and pinched doctrine, based on a world of total scarcity, to students who are, after all, relatively affluent. Its teachers repeatedly present a view of life that

can only be called hungry. Thus, a sex education lecturer
says:

> You have had practice in controlling your impulses and feelings
> ever since you have been a baby. By the time you get to be a
> high school senior, you don't eat all the chocolate cake you
> want to because you don't want to get fat. You do your home-
> work whether you want to or not. You take your college
> boards even if you don't feel like it that day . . . you don't steal
> clothes . . . . You have learned by now that it's part of being
> human, that you can't have what you want when you want it.

Hopes and dreams are deflated, those of parents as
well as students. I felt tugged in different directions watching an interview between parents and a counsellor. The
father is ambitious for his daughter, perhaps too ambitious.
A teacher had called some of her essays "fabulous," then
flunked her. The sententious counsellor explains it all to
the father, whose eyes glitter with frustration: "The total
mark involves more than just these papers. . . . We can only
judge on the basis of performance. You may have hidden
talent . . . but if you don't perform we don't know." "True,
true," the defeated man whispers. The counsellor spins out
some pop psychology and asks the daughter if she feels
guilty for letting her father down. "You cannot impose
preconceived values and dreams on an individual," he tells
the father. All very true, and a school can help protect kids
from pushy parents, but why, one wonders, is the message
at Northeast so insistent, and why is there so much bitter
joy in the work of denial? At least the father imagines
possibilities for the girl; the school is quick to snuff out
visions. In another scene, a college counselor tells a girl she
can apply to all her dream colleges, but that she should
have a college of last resort, "if none of your dreams come
true." Again, sensible advice. But in Northeast, this begins
to sound suspicious. Too many people are insisting on de-

feat. "You can't undo the past," a counsellor says. "Even if somebody has made a mistake and been wrong and unfair, you can't undo the past." In its setting, this bit of wisdom rings tinny. Sometimes parents collaborate with the school in teaching such lessons, as when a mother tries to get the school to assert an authority she has clearly lost over her defiant daughter.

The school asks little from the students, as teachers keep saying. Order is the main thing, and most students seem to find it easy to pay homage to order, even when they are openly insulted. A girl has it explained to her how wearing a short dress to the prom is an "insult" to the school. She must learn to abide by the standards of the majority. (The majority is constantly invoked.) "I think it's nice to be individualistic, but there are certain places to be individualistic," the teacher says. Under pressure, near tears, the girl recants, "I didn't mean to be individualistic."

Promiscuity cannot be tolerated, of course. You expect that in a high school. What is unexpected is the constant attack on students' sexuality. "This young lady, she's got a leg problem, too," a teacher says to a group of girls modeling a fashion show. Another shot of the same teacher shows her counting off girls' calisthenics; "Oh boy, are we feminine." The boys' sex lecture is an equally vulgar, and perhaps in the right sense of the word, dirty performance.

Northeast teaches the standard subjects. You might as well be in a wax museum. Occasionally the world intrudes: boys spend 193 hours in simulated space flight—a pointless enterprise, and they seem to take it in the right aimless spirit. A teacher discusses the history of labor relations: in the early days there was too little communication between capital and labor. A social studies teacher talks about Michael Harrington's *The Other America* and levels of poverty in America, and asks the class how many would join a

club that had Negro members—"there's no right or wrong
answer, I'm just trying to determine attitudes." There is an
inane music class. In one incredible scene, an English
teacher reads "Casey at the Bat" out loud to stupefied
students.

When you do see good teaching, you wonder if the
students know the difference. The language classes are lively, for example, but the students' faces aren't. A teacher
plays a Simon and Garfunkel record to a poetry class. She
lays down a smokescreen from the academy—"image, setting, figurative language, thematic words"—but she is really
trying, and the music is lovely. ("Dangling Conversation.")
The timing of this scene is extraordinary: by now you're
feeling so bleak inside, the music comes as a balm. The
camera lingers questioningly on the faces of the kids, but
their faces are mysterious, and you have no way of fathom-
ing what they make of this—some decent teaching about
something interesting, for a change. Deliberately, Wiseman
confines himself to what the school elicits from the students. We have no way of knowing what they really feel
about the school. It is entirely possible that they are as
complacent about it as the staff, even though it bores
them. Maybe, after all, they are learning the main lesson:
don't expect much. Perhaps their passivity is a necessary
defense: school can be survived, the way draftees endure
the army. You have to keep reminding yourself that it isn't
fair to ask for rebels or heroes: these are just kids, trying
to make sense of the world they're given, to fit in. In a
way they are too busy growing up to notice how bad the
school is. Years later, when they're adults, life might be
different. You don't know.

There is a handful of exceptions at Northeast—
troublemakers with long hair, shades, and even some beads.
Like other schools, it handles them by forming them into a

"human relations" society. A teacher presides, trying to get
them to take a more balanced view of the school. At last,
some student voices: "I think in its attitude toward education, its relations with the world today, this school is miserable. It's cloistered, it's secluded, it's completely sheltered
from everything that's going on in the world." Another,
conservatively dressed black student concedes that the science program is good, but "morally, socially, this school is
a garbage can."

High School should be seen for its own merits; it will
surely become a weapon in the war of life styles and classes
dividing America. Many will insist that the reason Northeast
is such a mournful place is that it institutionalizes the attitudes of a repressed lower-middle class. There is some truth
to this. But it's only part of the story. In a grim scene, a
teacher reads a letter from a soldier in Vietnam about to go
on a dangerous mission. If he gets killed, he'll leave his
insurance money to the school. He doesn't matter, he says,
he's "only a body." Northeast has probably had something
to do with convincing him that he's only a body, but it has
also given him loyalties: he loves the school. The fact that
his loyalties have been perverted into serving in a mon-
strous war doesn't make his letter any less moving.

One of the great obstacles to changing schools and
other institutions is the contempt the emancipated middle
class and its children feel for the straight middle- and
lower-middle class. The feeling is mutual, of course. But it
is particularly exasperating to see radicals and reformers
diverted from an attack on institutions to an attack on the
people trapped in them. Baiting teachers and the police,
denying that they are people, too, is becoming common, a
senseless as well as a morally ugly practice. By and large
the teachers at Northeast seem personally less repressive,
kinder, and even more sexy than the total ethos of the

institution they serve. (Although they are sentimental about the real functions of the school.) This is what has to be explained.

Northeast is no worse than other schools in America. It is probably better—at least its graduates are ready for college. Its main defect is that it isn't a school at all, in the sense of being a place where people learn important things about the world: it teaches students that they are just bodies, going through motions, getting by. The teachers are constantly appealing for denial and restraint but are unable to explain the purpose of all this sacrifice. The old appeals to uplift and purpose aren't working. The kids sit, glassy-eyed. Nothing seems to reach them. No single reform, no sweeping act of revolution will change this. A condition of the spirit is hard to cure.

Who Should Teach?

One difficulty in imagining alternatives to the way the professions are organized is the sheer complexity of so much of our social machinery. The education profession is an intricate apparatus of historical accident, neglect, and professional greed, loosely bound together by haywire and red tape, and since we seldom question the supposed necessities under which educators labor, it is not odd that in the past few of us wondered whether things had to be run the way they are. Today, however, a certain amount of critical intelligence is being applied to all the professions. There are even some signs of criticism of our strange system for licensing school teachers and administrators.

Present certification practices are absurd: they don't protect children from incompetent and unfit teachers and administrators; they don't guarantee a decent level of teaching; they don't provide incentives to good teachers and administrators; and they keep people out of schools who might do a better job than some of the professionals. State certification laws are partly to blame, but schools of education are more to blame. In general, ed-school training goes beyond state requirements in the number of worthless courses in non-subjects it demands. There are two useful things a prospective teacher can get from a training program. The first, especially for secondary school teachers, is knowledge of a subject like English or math. The second is supervised experience in practice teaching. Yet most ed schools continue to pile on more and more "education" courses, neglecting practice teaching which for all too many students turns out to be a lonely, unpleasant, and profitless exercise.

The greatest power the graduate schools of education have is their control over the programs for school administrators, for administrators dominate our over-administered school systems. (New Haven has an administrator for every nine classroom teachers.) No one can be considered for a job as principal or superintendent without years of graduate study in education, and often a candidate has to have a degree in educational administration. In many parts of the country, academic despots in the field hand-pick—for handsome consultant fees—all the nominees a board of education considers when it's choosing a new superintendent. Yet there is no body of knowledge called "education," nor any genuinely scholarly discipline called "educational administration." There is teaching experience, which ought to count for something, but schools of education do not give their full professorships to able, experienced teachers. Classroom teachers have almost no influence on teacher education. As I suggested earlier, this situation may be changing: the rise of powerful teachers' unions in big cities has led to a decline in the strength of school administrators, and the unions may now take an interest in reshaping training programs. If the unions can transcend their narrow guild mentality, if they can make peace with the embittered urban minorities, and if their leaders can avoid turning into a new class of educational bureaucrats, they may press for training programs with less of a mandarin cast, putting more emphasis on actual classroom experience. Monopolists infrequently are trust-busters, however, and I suspect that reform of the system will have to come from outside the educational profession, which has grown remote from the concerns of the rest of us.

Making professions and bureaucracies more responsive to their clients and to the public interest, making big institutions like school systems, hospitals, and universities more accountable—these are issues that will take us very far down winding roads. For the schools, a small first step toward a credentialling system that serves the public might be something like a recent piece of legislation in California that became law in the summer of 1970. There has been much debate over credentials. In 1961, after a controversial report by a California citizens' advisory council, an act called the Fisher Bill was passed over the resistance of hundreds of education lobbyists. It was intended to discourage teachers from majoring in education in college and to encourage them to take courses in the subjects they were to teach. The bill also reflected a belief that administrators should be reasonably broadly educated, having a solid background in classroom teaching—not just ex-coaches and home economics teachers with education degrees.

On paper, the Fisher Bill promised a big change; actually, it has been an administrator's nightmare. What was meant to be a simple set of guidelines became, as the state educational bureaucracy interpreted it, an incredibly complicated set of rules detailing all manner of acceptable university programs for teachers. A prospective teacher in California has the devil's own time knowing whether his transcripts of academic record meet these mysterious standards or not; the only way to find out is to mail them in and let the state's gnomes decide. The confusion was compounded by a teacher shortage in the state.

One purpose of the bill is to bring order out of chaos, to set up new rules simple enough to work. Another is to take licensing out of the hands of the education establishment and make it the responsiblity of classroom teachers and laymen. The bill establishes a permanent Commission on Teacher Preparation and Licensing consisting of working teachers and laymen—not "educators." Its members are chosen by the governor from a list compiled by the state department of education. Six are school people, four of whom must be full-time classroom teachers; four are college or university professors; two, members of local school boards; and three, private citizens. The monopoly of the ed schools on licensing is, in theory at least, broken.

Under this bill, a candidate for a teaching job needs a B.A.—not in education—and one of two things, either a graduate degree (which may be an education degree, but doesn't have to be) or a passing mark in an examination in the subject he wants to teach. If the subject exam is passed, no graduate degree would be needed. A teacher can take as many different exams as he wants. Within seven years after being hired, a new teacher has to do a fifth year of graduate study; the requirements are such that most people can fulfill them in summer school. In effect, the proposed teaching requirements enable any college graduate who passes a test to qualify immediately for a teaching job. And they immediately qualify almost anyone with a graduate degree in a reasonable field.

Requirements for administrators, principals, superintendents, and such are also fairly straightforward. Besides teaching credentials, an applicant has to have three years of full-time classroom experience in public or private schools, and he needs either to pass an administrator's exam approved by the commission, or to complete a program in school administration approved by the commission. The commission can approve training programs for administrators offered by local school districts or any accredited university, as well as the usual programs offered by the education schools.

A "grandfather" clause waives the new requirements for teachers and administrators now working in the system, as well as for people still in training.

The commission is charged with encouraging university departments—all of them, not just the ed school—to set up programs with local school systems, placing graduate students and undergraduates in classrooms as aides and assistants, and working out career lines for paraprofessionals. The object is to get the widest variety of school intern programs for teachers and administrators, programs run by school systems and university departments as well as the ed schools.

The California bill is anything but revolutionary. Its reliance on exams in the standard university subjects dodges any consideration of what makes an effective teacher, or whether the conventions of the credentialling economy are appropriate to the world of education. It skates on very thin ice over the whole matter of testing. Test scores in "hard" subjects like math and science may measure a person's knowledge, but objective tests in "soft" fields like English are something else; they easily degenerate into the kind of one-upmanship candidates used to encounter in Boston's notoriously shabby-genteel teachers' exam, where it helped to know the works of poets like Sara Teasdale.

Some testing is inevitable, no doubt, but it is hard to see how an exam for administrators will ever be anything but a subject for satire. And although the bill says its test won't discriminate against minorities, seeing is believing. California tradition has it that the legislature always tries to spell out the people's will in elaborate detail; it would be better if decisions in the tangled realm of testing should be left to the common sense of the teachers and laymen on the Commission.

A Massachusetts bill that died in legislative committee in the spring of 1969 was similar to the California bill, except that it very sensibly left testing procedures up to the members of the proposed licensing board. Important matters such as testing are, in this society, so often shaped by the mindless play of social forces or the machinations of self-interested professional groups. It would be refreshing for once to see them turned over to the sustained consideration of representatives of the public. The proposed Massachusetts bill made its intentions in this respect clearer than the California legislation did. (Similarities in the two bills are no accident—both were much influenced by the writings of James Koerner, a long-time critic of the education establishment.)

Now, it is the snobbish fashion of university professors to ridicule subjects taught in education courses. Many are a waste of time, but there is no evidence that the more respectable university disciplines are any better preparation for teaching, at least in primary schools. An M.A. in English does not necessarily make you any better at teaching reading. Even in secondary school teaching we ought to examine the claims of the academy with a cold eye, endeavoring to discover what advanced degrees from our universities actually mean. Many softer disciplines have little intellectual cohesion. Apart from a common core or narrow

technical training, graduate fields like English or history
are mainly categories that exist because university professors have a vested interest in the graduate school's depart-
mental system. They do not necessarily represent coherent
intellectual wholes. One small source of the malaise in our
universities is the manner in which narrow graduate disciplines have been permitted to dominate the entire intellectual life of the academy. Liberal arts degrees in the more
prestigious colleges have already turned into mini-Ph.D. programs, and the waves of this trend are washing over people
in crack high schools. I'm not saying that the universities
don't have anything to offer the schools or that teaching
wouldn't be better if more teachers knew more about the
subjects they were teaching. I am saying that the institutional priorities of the academy are far removed from con-
siderations of good teaching; most first-grade teachers give
more thought than most university professors to whether
their charges are following the lesson.

The authors of the California bill appear to have been
aware of all this. In different parts of the bill, they are
obviously straining toward more flexibility against the routine academic boundaries, trying to encourage interdisciplin-
ary B.A.s and so on. For primary school teachers, the subject exams would test general knowledge in broad areas—
the humanities or science. A strong Commission might at
some later date experiment with alternative paths to the
B.A., as well as teachers' certification. Two sleepers buried
in the bill could in theory mean a wholly different approach to licensing and credentialling. On the recommendation of a local school board, the commission has the power
to issue what is called a "subject credential" to anyone
who has achieved "eminence" in a field taught in the
schools. Interpreted liberally, this establishes a claim to
teach for all sorts of people who ought to be in schools—

artists, craftsmen, dancers, writers, engineers, professionals, social workers, retired people, people who want to work full- or part-time. Similarly, if a local board so recommends, the Commission can issue an "administration credential" to anyone whose experience is such that he would make a good principal or superintendent—in theory opening up these jobs to businessmen, college deans, and directors of community action programs, to name a few.

Whether the two sleepers will come to life depends partly on the power of the commission, but even more on the imagination and initiative of local communities. The most promising aspects of this bill rest on faith that some communities are interested in a different kind of schooling, and that a varied assortment of citizens can be persuaded to take a hand in the education of children. No one can predict how the bill will actually be administered, or how independent the commission will be of entrenched interests and old habits of mind. Nevertheless the bill is a great advance over the present system of licensing schoolmen. It offers alternative paths into the schools; it validates many different kinds of knowledge as a suitable background for teaching, and it opens up the schools to new kinds of talents. It does not solve all the problems raised for education by the credentialling economy, but nobody has solved them. At least it sets up a forum where they can be discussed in the light of ongoing experience.

Some people will be troubled by the fact that support for bills of this kind cuts across customary political and educational lines. Here, the party of reform is an alliance of those who want to weaken the grip of administrators, education schools, and state education establishments on our schools. In this sense, it represents an attack on the education profession, although it will undoubtedly win the support of many classroom teachers and people in the better

schools of education. It would not do to idealize the motives or talents of the motley forces backing this sort of
reform. Our schools, beset by crisis as they are, represent a
major growth industry; American education is a battleground on which various interests are struggling for power,
money, and control, against entrenched but increasingly insecure bureaucrats and administrators. Teachers' unions and
the urban minorities have been for some time the most
vocal contenders, but there are new groups, too: along with
sour-bellied populists and right-wing critics are government
and foundation people, university professors, urbanologists,
edbiz and knowledge industry magnates. These latter groups
tend to rally under the banners of the academy; they don't
necessarily speak for better or more humane schools; their
complacencies are not necessarily preferable to those of the
educators. Nor is there evidence that the newcomers are
any more knowledgeable about children or teaching or any
less corrupt than the groups whose grasp on the schools is
now loosening. Yet the entry of these new forces opens up
possibilities for releasing new energies in education. As in
California, people can band together in citizens' groups to
make the situation in the schools a little more fluid, a little
less ridiculous.

Technology and Schools

A footnote to modern learning is provided by a very
funny report that sprinkles cold water on extravagent
claims put forth for educational technology and "innovation" by gimcrack prophets and the hustlers from the edbiz
industries.* Its authors, Anthony Oettinger and Sema
Marks, have worked extensively with computers; Oettinger

*Anthony Oettinger and Sema Marks, *Run, Computer, Run*, Harvard University
Press, 1969.

is a professor of linguistics and applied mathematics at Harvard. They have surveyed current experimental programs which use hardware of one kind or another—particularly language laboratory equipment and computers, and conclude that much of this "innovation," far from freeing teachers from routine, piles on more mechanical and clerical work: testing, recording, setting things up, planning and maintaining schedules, storing and installing tapes or programs. The aim is to individualize instruction, but this is seldom the result. Protection of expensive equipment often takes precedence over learning—chewing gum is a major threat. The rigidities of the new order resemble those of the old: a lab manual says: "Students should be held responsible for laboratory work even if they have been barred from the laboratory work." Oettinger and Marks quote one set of laboratory rules: "No one is an individual in the laboratory."

The new technology is neutral toward such important matters as grading and grouping patterns; they continue unchanged. The extent to which existing computer-assisted instruction responds to individuals is minimal: most of the programs in use are just expensive page turners, mechanized versions of materials that could easily be put into a cheap programmed workbook. Theoretically, it's possible to create all sorts of complex, branching computer programs that can adapt to any number of responses from the student. In our present state of profound ignorance, however, it is hard for any programmer to anticipate more than a few simple alternatives. So the learner has to fit himself to the program, which is where we came in.

Reliability is essential, yet Oettinger and Marks offer many illustrations of how far away it is. It took a long time to develop washing machines, telephones, and cars that work more than fitfully, and it will probably take equally long to get instructional machines whose knobs don't fall off. And if we do develop serviceable machines, we may discover that they are too expensive for mass use. Estimates for a computer terminal, for example, range from $1.40 to $7 per pupil-hour. Oettinger and Marks don't anticipate anything like the mountain of cash that would be necessary for widespread computer instruction. There is no evidence for the proposition—dream for the social engineers, nightmare for teachers—that schools can save money by replacing teachers with computers. On the contrary, present experiments suggest that the advent of the computer and other new, complicated gadgets would create a demand for many more highly trained, higher paid specialists.

What is happening with computer learning is beginning to resemble what happened with programmed learning, which was also once thought of as the salvation of the education system. Like programmed materials, a few computer methods are beginning to look promising; many others don't. No great revolution has occurred. None seems likely. The computer technician's rule of thumb still holds good: GIGO. If you put garbage in, you get garbage out.

Oettinger and Marks, nonetheless, believe that the new technology does have a future, and they offer two examples. One is a college biology course that makes imaginative use of tapes and scheduling—and the energies of the excellent teacher. The other is some fascinating work with computers in math teaching, building geometric models of algebraic equations, projecting possibilities and alternatives in an open-ended way that actively engages the mind of the learner. (They don't mention O. K. Moore's "talking typewriter," which has always intrigued me, because children love it.) But if educational technology is to be taken out of the hands of the fools and frauds, they say, there will have

to be considerable further experimenting, financed on a
long-term basis, and involving working teachers, which few
current projects do. The folly of systems experts and cur-
ricular experts remote from the schools who attempt to
build a canned, teacher-proof curriculum is now apparent.
Yet conferences on implementing all the "innovations" continue to meet at tropical resorts; grants are proposed and
disposed of, and the legions of the great edbiz go marching
on.

Some years ago a number of educators and businessmen became attracted to the idea of applying to the mud-
dled field of education the precise techniques of planning—
system analysis and quantitative evaluation—that were believed to have been so successful in, of all places, the Department of Defense. The new edbiz industries were to be
modeled on the advanced defense and aerospace industries;
there was hope that profits, too, might be comparable. The
edbiz group assumed there were techniques, programmed
and computer materials, ready to replace traditional methods of teaching; the problem was dissemination. These
claims were largely promotional. For the systems approach
is generally inappropriate to education, where most of the
problems are human, not technical. Learning is far more
complex in its sequences and motives than the simple
models constructed by behaviorists, which are drawn from
observations of pigeons eating corn friskies, or people in
laboratory situations which lack all the variables of a classroom. As with so much military R&D, original exaggera-
tions in the edbiz have by now hardened into self-deception
and fraud.

Curiously, the enthusiasm for what can readily be
tested and measured has married the new scientism of the
behaviorists with the traditional scholastic verbalism of the
schools. For years, the vice of the schools was to teach

people to memorize strings of words instead of getting
them to think. The new technology is preoccupied with
what can be measured; and what can be measured, it turns
out, is the possession of strings of words. So much for the
study of human "behavior."

Run, Computer, Run documents another example of
the American hunger for simple technological solutions to
complex human problems. Oettinger and Marks dimly see
the possibility of a humane technology in the schools, and
so do I. In a profound little book called *The Teacher and
the Machine*, Philip W. Jackson reminded us that the threat
is never simply from technology; machines are neutral. The
threat is people capable of treating other people as
machines. School systems are already treating students and
teachers as though they were machines. That, not technology, is the source of our troubles, and that is what has to
change.

Kentucky Fried Children

In 1940, one mother in ten worked; the 1970 census
figures show that almost five in ten are working. Clearly an
enormous social change is occurring, and every sign points
to a permanent trend. Precise figures are impossible to ob-
tain, but it looks as though there are something like five
million children under six years old with working mothers.
How these children are taken care of is an immense, fright-
ening question. The highest estimate for the number of day
care places available is 640,000, and there are reasons for
thinking that figure too generous. For one thing the overwhelming number of day care establishments won't take
children under three; yet there are probably more than
1,600,000 children under three in need of care.

Depending on which experts you listen to, there are,

then, services in some form for between three and fifteen percent of the children needing them. The parents of the rest must make other arrangements. Some children stay home all alone. Some are with a relative, often an older brother or sister. Some are in what is called family care, lodged for the day in the house or the apartment of a neighbor, who takes in several youngsters and charges a fee. If everyone is lucky, this means safe care by somebody who really enjoys children. A general notion of what family care is like is hard to get. For every horror story, there are tales of good, kindly neighbors who go to great lengths for children. The few surveys that have been attempted do not suggest an encouraging picture, at least in our cities. Some years ago, the Medical and Health Research Association of New York City did a study of unlicensed homes, dealing with 25,000 of the city's children, half of them under six. The study found babies left completely unattended all day and caretakers who were drunks. A general hazard the report uncovered was that many people undertake to do family care because they are sick in one way or another and can't hold down other jobs. Even under good circumstances, the report showed, the day's schedule for the children is apt to be breakfast, TV, lunch, a nap, and then more TV. At a quarter of the homes surveyed, children were never once taken out to play; a third lacked any sort of materials or toys to play with; and four out of five were rated as inadequate, either because they violated the (perhaps excessively finicky) New York Health Code, or, more seriously, because in one way or another the children were neglected.

That is probably roughly the way most city children fare in family care, which Congresswoman Shirley Chisholm calls "custodial parking lots." What about licensed day care? I visited a number of ordinary day care facilities in

Washington, D.C. What I saw was no statistical sample; it was selected for me as typical of for-profit centers by Virginia Williams, the Washington official responsible for inspecting day care places.

The first place we visited was a new church building with a vast basement room and plenty of space for all kinds of activities with children. In a corner of this huge room, with all the curtains pulled, forty to fifty 2½-, 3-, 4-, and 5-year-olds huddled in even rows of chairs in the darkness, watching television. That was how they were going to pass the sunny summer day, even though outside the church there was a perfectly good fenced area for play, and across the street was one of the excellent D.C. public playgrounds. The basement room had some climbing apparatus and construction equipment, but it was all stored away in a corner, and it seemed likely that nobody had ever used it.

The next center was an apartment in a complex. When we arrived, all the children were swarming out in the parking lot in front of the building. There was no place else for them to play. The rather small apartment housing the center had flooded, and the man hadn't come to fix the floors. There was no aide, no toys nor equipment nor, indeed, anything else in the empty place. Asked about lunch, the woman in charge said she thought maybe today she would take the children down to a People's Drugstore for a hot dog. A suspicion crossed my mind that some days lunch just might not be served. I don't know this, of course; it was on my mind because I'd just been talking to someone who had visited a center in the city where lunch consisted of a little tinned fruit and two ounces of milk. As we left, one of the little girls had skinned her knee in the parking lot, and she was crying.

Another apartment-center made more of an effort. Two energetic women presided, and although there were only a handful of kids—in summer a lot of Washington children go back·to visit relatives in the South, which is probably a pretty good kind of day care—the center was pleasant. Some thought· had been given to providing materials and work space. There was a little handkerchief-sized plot for the children to play in.

The director at another center was ambitious: she was remodeling the whole house as a day nursery school. There was a playground in back, a good cook, and a pleasant staff. The director was desperate for somebody with experience working with young children to help her untrained aides develop some kind of a program.

Another church basement was an excellent site: big airy Sunday school classrooms, outfitted with all sorts of materials by a director who had run programs for children before. Staffing, again, was a problem: the aides were working with kids pretty much in the fashion of formal elementary school teachers, big groups, everybody quiet, seated for long periods at a stretch. In the play kitchen, the toys were neatly locked away in the cabinets.

All this is not exactly what I expected. There is nothing, at least in what I saw, to compare with what often gets reported about both licensed and unlicensed centers in many cities: children made to memorize hymns and complicated verses solely to impress parents, or children beaten, abused, or tied up for the day. With one exception, the people in charge of these places look well-intentioned, and two centers have the potential to do some worthwhile things with their kids. I wasn't too surprised at the general absence of toys, books to look at, or materials, or that there is too little space and that space is never used. What really astonished me was that reasonably pleasant adults are so totally incapable of thinking of things for themselves and the children to do, even to pass away an eight- to eleven-hour day. Scarcely any adult I saw even talked to a child. The children are universally bored to stupefaction. At two, three, four, and five,—all incredibly active years—they have the inert look of children in the later years of elementary school. Even when they aren't made to sit still, they remain for the most part oddly inactive and passive.

Virginia Williams inspects these places in order for them to keep their licenses, but she says she has no really effective authority to enforce standards. (This is true in many cities.) The machinery for closing down a rotten center is totally unwieldy. In any case, those offering day care know that they are in a seller's market. They don't need to pay much attention to parents' complaints, they can exclude unruly children, and, increasingly in Washington, they feel free to reject welfare parents in favor of better-heeled customers. Closing down a few centers would make little difference to the others, so, according to Virginia Williams, an inspector's time is better spent trying to upgrade what exists. She is impresive; she has a lot of experience with children, and she is improving things some.

People operating licensed for-profit centers are in the day care business to make a living, not because they are interested in children. (To judge by results, it looks to me as though they are less able to work with children than many of the parents they are serving.) They readily admit they know nothing about materials or activities, and they seem grateful for Virginia Williams's help. She says some will spend money on stuff—what exists now in these largely bare places was purchased at her urging. Many, she thinks, would take advantage of some sort of flexible early-childhood training program, if it were practical and, especially, if it could in some way be made part of licensing requirements. An inspectorate, several more Virginia Williamses, would be a great help, in part to maintain all the standards now so obviously honored in the breach—particularly on staff-to-children ratios—but more to assist some of the promising places to train people and develop halfway decent programs for their children. Like many with experience in early childhood teaching, Virginia Williams does not believe that these for-profit centers can ever offer good programs, because good programs cost too much.

In Washington, fees to the for-profit centers run around $15 to $20 a week. They charge less for an extra brother or sister from the same family. This is, of course, a fortune to poor families; and a steep price for the middle class, too.

The places I visited varied enormously in their budgets, and so, with the help of some figures compiled by the nonprofit National Capital Day Care Association, I'm going to suggest a composite budget for a D.C. center with forty children and a total income of $35,000 a year.

D.C. regulations say there has to be an adult for every ten children. (Remember, these are *little* children, two-and-a-half and up.) Leaving the director aside, then, you need a staff of three people. Let's pay them very low salaries, $3,000 a year, which makes $9,000.

Space might be free, but Headstart and other programs have used up most of the suitable church basements and sites, so rent will cost around $250 a month or a total of $3,000.

Buying very, very cheap food for forty children may cost as low as $2,800.

These centers don't spend much on equipment: a generous estimate would be $200.

Transportation is expensive: $6,000.

Thus total expenses in this first budget come to about $21,000, not counting the director's salary. If you are the owner of the center and act as your own director, that leaves a possible salary and profit for you of $14,000. If on

the other hand, the director is an employee, he probably
has to be paid more than the aides (for one thing, he has
the difficult job of meeting parents), so figure on giving
him $6,000. This leaves a possible profit for someone of
$8,000.

This is already a bare-bones budget for an operation
that might run an eleven-hour day. It can, however, be
trimmed further in the interests of profit. As parents get
more and more desperate for some kind of day care, it is
possible to make them pay extra for transportation, often
through the nose. So let's leave out transportation from our
budget. Also let's not have a director to supervise things;
let's just hire another underpaid aide for $3,000. Now we
have a profit of $17,000 or $20,000 from an income of
$35,000. To make such a profit you have to have inexperi-
enced aides without anybody to work with them, little equipment, and meals of beans and bread.

Suppose, however, like some of the people Virginia
Williams and I visited, you wanted to run a decent show.
You don't want to gouge parents by charging extra for
transportation, so you take care of that. And suppose you
are lucky enough to find a reasonable director willing to
work hard for $6,000. You add two more (underpaid) aides
to the staff, because you understand that three or four
adults can't possibly do a good job of working with forty
small children all day. Also, you try to serve adequate
food: a nonprofit day care center in Washington spends
$7,000 a year to feed forty-five children breakfast, lunch,
and two snacks; this sounds like a lot of money, but it
averages a thrifty sixty cents a day per child. You can't go
quite that far, but you are willing to add $2,000 more to
our original, miserable $2,800 food budget. By now, when
you add all this up, you find that your profits are approaching zero. The squeeze is very tight.

Speculation about budgets is, of course, only speculation. A budget is only a framework in which good or bad things can take place. Such exercises as I've been going through don't take into account regional variations in labor costs, and they certainly don't allow for special circumstances or particularly dedicated or energetic people. Day nurseries with a middle-class clientele and a lot of volunteer labor manage good, cheap programs. So do parent cooperatives. In many places were are small numbers of good centers run by director-owners whose only financial goal is a fairly modest salary. All I have tried to show is the plausibility of a certain rule of thumb about the finances of day care operations: a great deal of profit can be made from a rotten program, whereas the bare essentials of a decent program soon run you into or very close to the red. This is no iron law, but it tends to hold for all sorts of people in the business, including those who might be assumed to have good, or at least respectable, intentions. Many church groups in Washington run appalling day care operations in the basements of their newly acquired church buildings; they started them in order to pay off the mortgage, and now they find that financial pressure and an adequate program are incompatible. Their response to this discovery depends on their degree of Christian concern for the children; a few have made efforts to improve.

The great, immovable expense in day care for young children is a high ratio of adults to kids. Small children can be made to sit all day, like elementary school children, but it is a difficult art, requiring constant adult monitoring. Thus even when day care centers try to adopt the group-teaching, labor-saving methods of the schools, they find they need more hands. More are needed whether they are good or bad with children. To be good, it is increasingly evident, people don't need a lot of elaborate degrees; but they need experience with young children, and preferably work experience in good preschool settings, so they have some idea of what sort of atmosphere and activities are appropriate for children. These days, with the expansion of preschooling, it is extremely unlikely that you would get such experienced people to stay if you paid them $3,000 and asked them to work eight to eleven hours a day. These long hours pose particular problems. Even the best non-profit centers have to fight to keep the staff fresh and the responses to the children unstereotyped; in most elementary schools, after all, teachers' tongues are hanging on the floor by three in the afternoon. To solve this problem day care centers must pay so that no teacher works more than eight hours a day; sometimes the extra staffing can cost half again as much in basic salaries.

There is always astonishment when day care people insist that good care costs around $2,000 to $3,000 a year per child—more than twice the going rate in the for-profit D.C. centers. (Headstart, which often runs much shorter hours than ordinary day care programs, now costs about $2,000 a year per student.)

It seems to me wildly implausible that we will get this kind of money for day care on any big scale for a long time, if ever, but it is really not an inflated figure. Part of the cost is paying professionals to work with uncredentialed, if often experienced, people. But the professionals in day care get fairly modest salaries, and everyone is at the point of agreeing that day care teachers don't need early-childhood degrees. (However, the career ladders by which paraprofessionals can become teachers still seem to be missing a good many rungs.) Good nonprofit programs also include medical and dental care for the children, which costs a good deal, but which is also terribly important.

The question of what constitutes good standards of day care, and how we get more of it is going to become more and more pressing. The Congress is awash with day care proposals. Senator Walter Mondale has proposed a bill that would expand many varieties of early childhood education, including day care; so would another thorough and well-conceived bill offered by Representative John Brademas. Representatives John Dellenback and Ogden Reid have a bill, as does Senator Winston Prouty. Senator Russell Long has proposed a federal "Child Care Corporation" whose exact workings nobody understands, but its purpose would be to expand day care for children of working parents.

There were substantial day care provisions in the Nixon Administration's welfare reform package, which has now been shelved for a year. Its proposals are not primarily aimed at benefiting children; they are an attempt to get mothers off the welfare rolls. Under the bill, mothers with children over six would be forced to accept day care for them, and to enroll in job or training programs. Nonetheless, the bill would allocate $386 million to be spent on some (vaguely defined level of care for 150,000 preschool and 400,000 school-age children.

All these bills, but particularly the Nixon Administration's possible extension of day care, attracted the attention of a number of new businesses springing up to cultivate what many believe to be a national market for various kinds of child services. A few are fired by the vision of federal largess for services to welfare mothers. Some are more interested in the possibility of an expanding middle-class market. In fact, most actual, working commercial centers cater to parents well above the poverty line. The level of investment in research and tentative promotion is much bigger than the level of actual operations: most of the businesses remain fairly small, local operations.

Some are marketing franchises for child care the way

others have sold franchises for root beer and fried chicken. Franchisers like Kinder Care Nurseries and the American Child Care Centers Inc. are opening up centers, especially in the South where the level of both preschool public services and wages are scrawny. Customers who buy franchises pay from $18,000 (Mary Moppet in the Southwest) to $30,000 (American Centers), along with a continuing fee of about six percent of gross sales. Construction and other initial costs may require as much as $200,000 in capital for a start. The promised return is said, variously, to be between twelve and twenty percent, and purchasers of franchises hope to earn from $25,000 to $50,000. Fees to parents are $20 to $30 a week.

Since most good nonprofit day care costs around $40 a week, the nonprofit day care orthodoxy is deeply suspicious of Kentucky Fried Children. I share their suspicion. I don't think the franchisers will be able to make money running good programs. At best, they will provide pleasant, expensive baby-sitting services for children, not an educational program. Much of their present talk is what a social scientist might call fund-oriented, reminiscent of all the promotional hoopla in the middle sixties about the fortunes to be made in the edbiz. The most careful market survey I've seen suggests that, barring federal subsidies, there is no safe market for selling day care in the inner cities or in the affluent suburbs. More likely prospects are lower-middle-class communities like Medford, Massachusetts, where more wives are working and community services remain very poor.

The entrance of the franchisers onstage is a reminder that there are scarcely any effective standards for services dealing with young children. It seems plausible that if companies cannot make money on good programs, they will have plenty of incentives to operate bad ones, as so many solitary entrepreneurs now do. How can the children be protected?

At the state and local levels, various committees and councils are at work trying to develop reasonable standards for day care. They are discovering that existing regulations are unenforceable—and that, without benefit of national franchises, local operators long ago discovered how to run overcrowded, lucrative programs. The situation on the local level reminds many people of battles some time ago in state legislatures to establish some sort of standards for nursing homes. These battles in most places were lost to nursing home interests which then went on to make fortunes out of federal Medicare and Medicaid windfalls without any improvement in their abysmal services. In many respects the analogy is intriguing: young children and old people suffer worst of any groups from the existence of age-ghettos in our society. Relatives of old people, like parents of young children, do not always know what a good program is and, in some cases, don't want to know. The complaints of the young and the old do not always get heard. The nursing home analogy is weak in one respect, however: there may never be as much money in child care as in supplying medical services, nursing care, and drugs to captive old people.

Both locally and nationally there is a need for inspectorates, experienced early-childhood people whose business it is to set practical standards and help people meet them. They ought to have authority to revoke licenses and close places down, but in the present condition of scarcity, they should shut them only for gross violations. In many places the physical requirements for facilities are inflexible and mainly benefit large institutions like the public schools; except for real dangers to health and physical safety, they should be enforced lightly. Ultimately there should be subsidies to good private programs, such as the KLH (an electronics firm) day care center in Cambridge, Massachusetts; it is particularly likely that labor unions and big institutions like hospitals will expand day care for their workers if some sort of federal subsidies are available.

The place where standards really need enforcing is on adult-to-child ratios. In order to get some national standards on staffing, the ratios set forth in the federal Inter-Agency Day Care Requirements should apply to all programs getting federal funds. These requirements state that for children from three to four, there should be a ratio of five children to one adult; from four to six, a ration of seven children to one adult. In the light of the very long revolution now beginning in credentialing, it would be a poor idea to set rigid standards, such as academic degrees.

The main function of the inspectorates would be staff development, setting up programs by which experienced people could qualify themselves in the field for higher positions. The inspectorates should establish day care centers in high schools where students can train for diplomas in infant and child care. Their purview should include training and standards for people engaged in home care, as well. The inspectors might well want to tie such training to existing, good group day care facilities, operating in the manner of some of the excellent Headstart parent and child centers dealing with mothers, fathers, and infants.

The nonprofit day care orthodoxy, like other small, protected realms of our preschool tradition, is getting badly shaken up. Group care was at one time a purely custodial, not an educational matter. It was a welfare measure for the benefit of the mother. Often, too, people offering non-profit group day care have been put in the position of having to administer our society's Poor Laws, which has meant that a certain amount of welfare paternalism has tinged their work. They have also been too steeped in middle-class nursery school traditions: children were to bloom like flowers, without much intellectual stimulation.

Many of these traditions are starting to change. The involvement of day care professionals and paraprofessionals in parent-controlled centers in Headstart programs and in places like New York has helped some of them shed their welfare mentality, the assumption, for instance, that mothers in need of day care are somehow social misfits. Some are breaking out of the stereotypes of the nursery schools, and are discovering that good teachers steal ideas from everywhere to make schools interesting environments.

The result is a number of good places, scattered over the map: storefronts, nurseries, day care centers, and Headstart operations that are excellent places for children to be, unlike most other facilities for children in this society, and *most* unlike the public schools. For all its weaknesses, then, and its tiny numbers in the face of vast needs, the early childhood orthodoxy has access to something that until recently was lacking to reformers in the schools: working models of what a good job looks like. In whatever way our early childhood programs expand, there should be an emphasis on training in such sites.

Day care, like all areas of early-childhood education, is nearly a vacuum. Whereas with the schools, the reformers' problem is to fight sick bureaucracies, pathological professionalism, and many other entrenched interests, the problem in early-childhood education is simpler and bigger: how to develop from a few shoots an entire new humane profession, responsible to its clients. And, of course, how to get hold of some money.